Living Crazy Healthy

PLANT-BASED RECIPES

JENNIFER ROSE ROSSANO
OF NEUROTIC mommy

GIBBS SMITH
TO ENRICH AND INSPIRE HUMANKIND

First Edition
22 21 20 19 18   5 4 3 2 1

Published by
Gibbs Smith
P.O. Box 667
Layton, Utah 84041

1.800.835.4993 orders
www.gibbs-smith.com

Designed by Mina Bach
Printed and bound in Hong Kong
Gibbs Smith books are printed on paper produced from sustainable PEFC-certified
forest/controlled wood source. Learn more at www.pefc.org.

This book is not intended to provide medical advice. All content, including text, graphics,
images, and information in this book is for general informational and educational purposes
only. The content in this book is not intended to be a substitute for professional diagnosis or
treatment. The author and publisher of this book are not responsible for any adverse effects
that may occur with the use of the information in this book. You are encouraged to make
your own healthcare decisions based on your research and in partnership with a qualified
healthcare professional.

Library of Congress Cataloging-in-Publication Data

Names: Rossano, Jennifer Rose, author.
Title: Living crazy healthy : plant-based recipes / Jennifer Rose Rossano.
Description: First edition. | Layton, Utah : Gibbs Smith, [2018] | Includes index.
Identifiers: LCCN 2018000345 | ISBN 9781423648710 (hardcover)
Subjects: LCSH: Vegan cooking. | LCGFT: Cookbooks.
Classification: LCC TX714 .R6746 2018 | DDC 641.5/636—dc23 LC record available at
https://lccn.loc.gov/2018000345

To my sons Michael and Oliver,

You're my forever inspiration.
My heart is your heart.

Love, Mom

To my husband Nestor,

I couldn't have done it
without you.
Thank you.
I love you.

♡

Contents

Acknowledgments

Thank you to Ginny and Doug from Erickson Woodworks for supplying me with the photography boards that are used throughout all my photos.

Thank you to MacKenzie, my literary agent, and Michelle, my editor, for guiding me and being on this adventure with me. You ladies have been true gems.

Thank you to Gibbs Smith for making dreams come true.

INTRODUCTION

"EATING HEALTHY ISN'T ABOUT RESTRICTION"

Growing up Italian and Puerto Rican, I had never even heard the words vegan or plant based. I didn't find out about this way of life until I was in my mid- to late twenties, and even then I didn't really comprehend what it meant. In my mind, vegans were crazy extremists who didn't eat meat. At the time, not eating meat—let alone any animal products—was absurd to me, and I didn't give it a second thought.

I chalk that up to being somewhat immature and not very open-minded. Eating healthy to me meant restricting calories, eating grilled chicken with green beans, salad without dressing, bland brown rice, and protein bars and shakes that tasted like cardboard boxes. Then there were the freezer meals from Lean Cuisine or Weight Watchers with burgers for three points and the smallest servings of pasta imaginable that you could just pop in the microwave and call it a night. Looking back, popping any food in the microwave is far from being healthy. (Not to mention all the foods that I thought were food, but were really just

chemical concoctions with very little to no nutrition at all.) I ate that crap and thought I was on the healthy track of life. Ah, well, you live and you learn, right? And thank God for that.

Boy, let me tell you, when I stumbled upon living a greener way of life and all the foods I hadn't a clue about, it was a whole new world for me. I couldn't believe I had never heard of almond meal, quinoa, or kale. I was so unaware of smoothies, juicing, or using spaghetti squash as pasta that I remember thinking, "I've been missing out on all this!?" It was super frustrating at first because not only did I not know about any of these foods or how to prepare them, but I had also gone most of my life without properly feeding myself. And I couldn't blame my family because they didn't know any better either. Lucky for me, and them, that was all about to change.

When I say, "stumbled upon," I really mean just that. You see, after I had my oldest son, I became a complete hypochondriac—but not the type that you can find humor in. The whole first year after my son was born, I was a complete anxious and depressed mess. I feared for everything: my life, my son's life, my family. My mind held me captive as prisoner for a good year, leaving me wondering why this was happening to me and what exactly was happening to me. I remember saying to my husband, "I'm going crazy. I was never like this. What is happening to me?" It was probably the toughest year of my life.

I was at a doctor's office almost four times a week for some appointment or another, absolutely certain something was wrong. I got every kind of test done, because I thought there was just no way there was nothing wrong with me. There had to be something. Minor aches and pains weren't minor to me. Having a pain in my leg that would be normal to anyone else, to me were blood clots, and I would soon die if the doctors didn't catch it in time. I would have my breasts checked,

my throat checked, my eyes checked, everything checked, because
I was living in fear that something bad was going to happen. And if
something bad happened to me, who was going to take care of my son?
As a mom, you know that no one will look after your baby the way you
do. No one will love your baby like you do, and this preyed on my mind
night and day.

I was definitely going through postpartum depression but hadn't a
clue at the time. Without proper help, I was spiraling out of control.
I needed to get my life back for the sake of myself and my family. I
remember going to see therapists and psychologists who wanted to put
me on a slew of medications, and I just felt there had to be a better
way. I didn't want to disguise what I was going through; I wanted to get
to the root cause of it and deal with it. I didn't want a mask. I wanted a
resolution—a final ending to this nightmare of fear I was living in. And
then I found it. I went through a true awakening.

I came across an article on Facebook about food and veganism. It
spoke about the correlation between food and gut health and how the
gut is basically our second brain. It went on to say how foods affect
your mood, what GMOs are, and how they are affecting society as
a whole. Everything the article talked about was what I was going
through, and I saw a ray of light. There it was—the beginning of my new
life—right in front of me. I knew a shift was coming, and it was all going
to be for the better. Oh, and it was.

My curiosity got the best of me, and I started researching. I was
reading any article I could find; watching every documentary there
was to learn as much as I could. I was introduced to holistic living,
plant-based eating, essential oils, homeopathic remedies, naturopaths,
shamanic healers, yoga, meditation, light workers, and the like. Once
I was on this path, it was like doors just kept opening for me left

and right and I was taking it all in. My doctor's appointments became fewer and fewer until they completely stopped. I wasn't afraid to go pumpkin picking with my family, and I started to frequent the beach in the summer. All of which I was afraid to do for a whole year because I didn't want anything "bad to happen."

Food is so huge for me because it's also tradition. You have holidays, birthdays, special occasions, and anniversaries where food always takes center stage. When you grow up knowing how to cook only one way, learning how to start all over again can be completely overwhelming and a bit frightening. When I first started cooking this way, there were nights that I had no idea what I, let alone my family, was going to eat.

I learned the difference between organic and GMO and started to only buy organic. It is true organic can be expensive, but you have to shop smart, which is something I learned along the way. So instead of buying vegetable oil, I bought coconut oil. Instead of buying cookies or sugary cereals, I opted for a bag of chia seeds and a container of rolled oats to make my own chia puddings and overnight oats. Instead of buying regular sugar, I chose maple syrup and coconut nectar. I started to replace the items I once purchased religiously with the healthier choices. And the next thing I knew, my entire kitchen was organic and plant based.

The more I learned, the more I would make changes. I realized that the things I was eating—for instance, chicken that's unethically raised—came with consequences. If those chickens were suffering in life, feeling depressed and scared, and I was eating them, the cells in those chickens were making up my body. My emotional distress was being enhanced by my poor food choices. You know the saying, "You are what you eat." Well, there's a better saying quoted from Dr.

Josh Axe: "You are what you digest." This means that if your body is filled with toxins and sludge, it won't be able to properly absorb the nutritious benefits of the foods that pass through your system. You have to have a green and clean inside to reap the benefits of the quality foods you do eat.

There are foods that take twenty minutes to pass through our system, like fruits and veggies, and then there are foods that can take up to six hours to digest—mostly meats and cheeses. These foods typically ferment and spoil while they are still in our digestive tracts, leading to very unpleasant gases, unwanted belly bloats, and even upset stomachs. In even more severe instances, problems like leaky gut, diverticulitis, Crohn's disease, and ulcerative colitis can occur.

When you're someone like me, who is basically a recovering hypochondriac *and* a new mom, you want to do whatever you can do that's the absolute best for you and your family. And rightfully so. This helped me heal, and by healing myself I am able to help people get on their own healing path. So I'm thankful for my struggles and the dark times I went through. They taught me my strengths and showed me a different way of life that I am now utterly grateful for.

Eating healthy isn't about restriction or deprivation for you or your family. It's not about getting rid of all foods you love. It's about finding a balance that works for you, and that works for your family. It's about knowing you can

eat real food without having to compromise taste, texture, or tradition. It's about knowing that what you're putting into your body is actually nourishing you and providing you with ample and sufficient energy you need throughout the day. You can still enjoy food. It's about being in a healthy relationship with food, leading you toward having a healthy relationship with yourself and connecting all aspects of life, mind, body, and soul.

Thank you for purchasing my book. My goal is not only to inspire you, but also to show you that cooking and eating healthy doesn't mean doing away with traditions, but perhaps creating new ones. It doesn't mean cooking all day and night in the kitchen, and it doesn't mean less fun and less taste. In fact, it's the complete opposite. It's about family time, learning, and having your kids be part of the process. Making meals that are so nutritious and mind-blowingly good that even your five year old can get in on the action—that's what it's about.

→| **Talk to your kids about the foods you eat.**

→| **Show them how each fruit or veggie has a different texture.**

→| **Let them feel it, let them smell it.**

Fruit will be sweeter and veggies will be better when your kids take an active role in preparing what they eat. Show gratitude while making anything because, like plants and like humans, your food will flourish and be even more nurturing when made with love.

This book is for parents and caretakers who need to understand that there's no reason to be intimidated about preparing healthy meals. I was overwhelmed in the beginning because I had no guidance. Now you have guidance, and the recipes! Oh, the recipes—classic, traditional recipes that will for sure be on weekly rotations. I went from only being able to butter toast and ice some cubes to making these delicious meals for my family, and I'm so, so happy I can share them with you!

There are endless possibilities to healthy eating. Each day poses new challenges for all of us. So, parents, don't be so hard on yourselves; we're all just doing the very best we can. Take from me, and this book, what will work for *you*. I promise you will be healthily full, and your kids will feel great both on the inside and the outside.

To get you started on your new cooking and eating adventure, I've provided you with a list of my favorite, and most used, kitchen tools, followed by a list of foods that I keep stocked in my kitchen all of the time, except for some of the fruits and vegetables that I buy as needed or when they are in season. You will develop your own lists of favorite tools and pantry items as you find your own way to living crazy healthy!

KITCHEN TOOLS AND EQUIPMENT

- Blender
- Cutting boards
- Food processor
- Glass bowls
- Hand mixer
- Knives
- Mason jars, for storing
- Rolling pin
- Rubber spatulas
- Stand mixer
- Wooden spoons
- Ziplock bags

WHAT'S IN MY PANTRY

Dry Ingredients

- All-purpose flour
- All-purpose gluten-free flour
- Almond flour
- Almond meal
- Baking powder
- Baking soda
- Brown rice flour
- Cashew meal
- Cocoa powder
- Coconut (shredded)
- Coconut flour
- Cornmeal
- Cornstarch
- Hazelnut meal
- Millet flour
- Rolled oats
- Spelt flour
- Tapioca flour
- Whole-wheat pastry flour
- Yeast

Oils

- Avocado oil
- Coconut oil
- Extra virgin olive oil
- Olive oil
- Safflower oil
- Sunflower oil

Grains

- Bulgur
- Couscous
- Kasha

- Millet
- Oats (rolled)
- Quinoa

- Rice, brown and white

Pasta (wheat, lentil, quinoa, and spelt options)

- Capellini
- Elbow macaroni
- Fettuccine

- Fusili
- Linguine
- Penne

- Rigatoni
- Spaghetti
- Ziti

Breads

- Multigrain bread
- Sprouted bagels

- Sprouted English muffins
- Whole-wheat bread

- Whole-white bread
- Wraps

Sweeteners

- Agave nectar
- Brown rice syrup
- Coconut nectar
- Coconut sugar
- Dates

- Maple syrup
- Monk fruit
- Organic cane sugar (white and light brown)

- Organic confectioners' sugar
- Stevia

If you are using cane sugar (organic or not), always look for a vegan certification. If you are unsure whether any product is vegan, make sure you read the ingredient list.

Condiments

- Agar-agar
- Almond extract
- Braggs Liquid Aminos
- Cacao nibs
- Chocolate chips (dairy free)
- Coconut aminos
- Coconut extract
- Coffee (decaf)
- Dark chocolate
- Ketchup
- Marshmallows (dairy free)
- Mustard
- Olives (black and green)
- Soy sauce (low sodium)
- Tamari sauce
- Tea
- Vanilla extract
- Vegan butter
- Vegan cheeses
- Vegan cream cheese
- Vegan mayonnaise
- Vegan sour cream
- Vegan salad dressings of choice
- Vegan shortening

Spices

- Basil (fresh and dried)
- Cardamom
- Cinnamon
- Cloves
- Dill (fresh and dried)
- Garlic powder
- Ginger (ground and fresh root)
- Marmite
- Mint (fresh and dried)
- Nutmeg
- Nutritional yeast
- Onion powder
- Oregano (fresh and dried)
- Parsley (fresh and dried)
- Pepper
- Pink Himalayan sea salt
- Rosemary (fresh and dried)
- Thyme (fresh and dried)
- Turmeric (ground and fresh root)

Dairy-Free Milks

- Almond milk
- Cashew milk
- Coconut milk
- Hemp milk
- Rice milk
- Soy milk

Fruits (fresh or frozen)

- Apples (different varieties)
- Bananas
- Berries (mixed)
- Blackberries
- Blueberries
- Cherries
- Dried fruits (raisins, dates, etc.)
- Figs
- Frozen acai
- Frozen pitaya (dragon fruit)
- Grapes (green or red)
- Kiwi
- Lemons and limes
- Mangos
- Melons (watermelon, honeydew)
- Oranges
- Papaya
- Peaches
- Pineapple
- Raspberries
- Strawberries

Vegetables (fresh or frozen)

- Acorn squash
- Cabbage
- Carrots
- Cauliflower
- Celery
- Collard greens
- Corn
- Cucumbers
- Eggplant
- Garlic
- Green beans
- Kale
- Microgreens
- Mushrooms (all varieties)
- Onions (red, yellow, and white)
- Peppers
- Potatoes
- Pumpkin
- Romaine lettuce
- Shallots
- Spaghetti squash
- Spinach
- Sweet potatoes
- Tomatoes (fresh and canned, tomato sauce, tomato paste)
- Zucchini

Beans and legumes

- Black beans
- Chickpeas / Garbanzo beans
- Lentils
- Pinto beans
- Red kidney beans
- Navy beans
- Tempeh
- Tofu

Nuts and Seeds

- Almonds
- Cashews
- Hazelnuts
- Macadamias
- Peanuts
- Pecans
- Pistachio
- Sesame seeds
- Sunflower seeds
- Walnuts

Nut and Seed Butters

- Almond butter
- Cashew butter
- Coconut butter
- Hazelnut spread
- Hummus
- Peanut butter
- Sunflower butter
- Tahini

Superfoods

- Acai powder
- Baobab powder
- Cacao powder
- Chia seeds
- Chicory root
- Flax seeds
- Goji berries
- Hemp seeds
- Maca powder
- Spirulina
- Plant-based protein powders (vanilla or chocolate)
- Wheat grass

Frozen

- Fruits and Veggies
- Ready-made cornmeal crusts
- Ready-made vegan pie crusts
- Ready-made vegan pizza crust

Where I Shop to Stay on Budget

- Local health food shop

- ShopRite
- Target

- Trader Joe's
- Whole Foods Market

Egg Substitute—Flax Egg

This is a great substitute for eggs to be used in recipes. One flax egg is the equivalent of a regular chicken egg.

To make 1 flax egg:

Mix together 1 tablespoon ground flax seeds and 3 tablespoons water. Let rest for a few minutes and then proceed just as you would with a chicken egg. Repeat to make however many eggs are required for the recipe.

BREAKFASTS

It's no secret that breakfast is the most important meal of the day. Breakfast is what gets your body going. By skipping breakfast you can set yourself up for unnecessary snacking during the day, or even worse, binge eating at night before bed. Not only is the first meal of the day uber important, but what you eat also matters because food impacts on your energy, concentration, cravings, attitude, and mood. Think brain food and heart health. Here are some tasty and simple breakfast recipes that will fuel and nourish your body the right way come morning.

BLUEBERRY CHEESECAKE FRENCH TOAST BAKE

Blueberries have quite the reputation for being one of the healthiest foods on earth. With blueberries in every bite, you'll be feeding your family high-quality amazingness serving this recipe. They'll certainly be coming back for seconds.

Serves 8

4 flax eggs (page 23)

1 cup almond milk

2 tablespoons cornstarch

2 teaspoons vanilla extract

2 tablespoons maple syrup, plus extra

8 slices organic white bread or bread of choice, cubed

Topping

1 cup fresh blueberries, plus extra

1/3 cup coconut sugar

Cinnamon, to taste

1/2 cup vegan cream cheese

Preheat oven to 350 degrees. Prepare an 8 x 10-inch baking dish with nonstick cooking spray.

In a medium bowl combine flax eggs, milk, cornstarch, vanilla, and syrup.

Layer the cubed bread in the bottom of baking dish. Pour milk mixture evenly over bread cubes, making sure the bread is completely soaked.

Topping

Sprinkle blueberries, sugar, and cinnamon evenly over the top, adding small dollops of cream cheese in a random pattern. Bake for 45–50 minutes. Remove from oven and let set for 5 minutes. To serve, cut into squares and drizzle with maple syrup and extra blueberries.

KID HELP

- Have your child rinse the blueberries while you prep.
- Give them the job of putting the cubed bread in the baking dish.
- Let your child dollop the cream cheese on, as it doesn't have to be perfect.

CHOCOLATE CHIP OATMEAL BAKE

Eating oatmeal in the morning is a great way to fuel up to stay full longer. Turning it into a bake and adding chocolate chips makes it so much fun. And besides, chocolate chips make everything better!

Serves 9

2 cups rolled oats

1 teaspoon baking powder

1 teaspoon baking soda

1 teaspoon cinnamon

Pinch of salt

$1\frac{1}{2}$ teaspoons vanilla extract

$\frac{1}{2}$ cup coconut sugar or brown sugar

$1\frac{1}{2}$ cups almond milk

2 tablespoons maple syrup

1 flax egg (page 23)

1 mashed banana

1 cup dairy-free chocolate chips

1 handful shredded coconut, optional

Icing Drizzle

1 cup organic powdered sugar

5 tablespoons almond milk

1 teaspoon vanilla extract

Dairy-free yogurt, optional

Preheat oven to 350 degrees. Prepare a 9 x 9-inch baking dish with nonstick cooking spray.

Place all ingredients except the chocolate chips and coconut in a large bowl and mix well. Fold in chocolate chips. Place mixture into baking dish and spread evenly over the bottom. Top with coconut, if using.

Bake for 30 minutes. Remove from oven and let cool for 5 minutes.

Icing Drizzle

Combine the ingredients together in a small bowl until mixed. Drizzle icing over the top and serve.

Note: Rather than drizzling with icing, you can also use yogurt. You can dollop it on top, or add some yogurt to a ziplock bag and cut off a small corner, and pipe on a design.

KID HELP

- Give your child some ingredients to add into the bowl then let them mix it up (as best they can). When they are done, you can give it a good whirl if needed.
- Have your child mash the banana—kids love mashing things!
- Let the kids drizzle the icing, and then lick the spoon!

PEANUT BUTTER OVERNIGHT OATS OR CHIA PUDDING

Peanut butter adds to the creamy texture of this breakfast. It is also high in vitamin E, so while it's fantastic to your taste buds, it's also keeping you looking good.

Serves 2

Overnight Oats

1 cup rolled oats

2 cups almond or coconut milk (I prefer unsweetened)

1 tablespoon maple syrup

1 tablespoon chia seeds

2 tablespoons strawberry or grape jelly, divided

4 tablespoons peanut butter, divided

1 handful roasted peanuts, optional

Chia Pudding

2 cups almond or coconut milk

6 tablespoons chia seeds

1 teaspoon vanilla extract

2 tablespoons maple syrup

2 tablespoons strawberry or grape jelly, divided

4 tablespoons peanut butter, divided

Overnight Oats

In a large Mason jar, mix together the oats, milk, syrup, and chia seeds. Refrigerate for up to 4 hours or overnight. This is where it will come together and become super creamy.

When ready to eat, divide oats into 2 serving glasses and place 1 tablespoon of jam and 2 tablespoons of peanut butter into each glass. You can parfait them into layers, or just mix it all together. Top with roasted peanuts for added crunch, if desired.

Chia Pudding

In a large Mason jar, mix together the milk, chia seeds, vanilla, and syrup. Refrigerate for up to 4 hours or overnight.

When ready to eat, divide pudding into 2 serving glasses and place 1 tablespoon of jam and 2 tablespoons peanut butter into each glass. You can parfait them into layers, or just mix it all together.

KID HELP

- As you're portioning the ingredients, hand them to your kids so they can add them to the jar.
- When everything is in the Mason jar, let them stir with a spoon then give it a good shake so it's well-incorporated.

BANANA-VANILLA OVERNIGHT OATS WITH CHIA SEEDS

Bananas are known to be high in potassium, but they're also really good at helping muscles grow and move well. So while they're sweet by nature, making everything taste delicious, they're even sweeter for helping our bodies function as they should!

Serves 2

1 cup rolled oats

2 tablespoons chia seeds

2 cups almond or coconut milk

2 mashed bananas

2 tablespoons maple syrup or any liquid sweetener, of choice

2 teaspoons vanilla extract

Dairy-free yogurt, optional

Fresh bananas, optional

Place oats, chia seeds, milk, mashed bananas, maple syrup, and vanilla into a large Mason jar and mix well. Seal with lid. Refrigerate for up to 4 hours or overnight.

When ready to eat, give it a good stir and add some yogurt and fresh bananas on top. You can also make a parfait with banana slices between layers of oatmeal.

 KID HELP

- Have your kids mash up some bananas. That's always a fun task.
- I like to let my son fill up a big bowl with all the ingredients then I let him stir it. Once he's done doing that, I transfer the mixture into Mason jars.
- Have your child pick out toppings for their bowl. I love coconut shavings, cacao nibs, almond butter, and fresh fruit!

EASY TOFU SCRAMBLE WITH TOAST

Organic tofu is super high in protein, and is a great scrambled egg replacement. The texture is almost identical and the addition of turmeric keeps the color just right. Turmeric is like the queen of spices, leaving traditional scrambled eggs in the dust.

Serves 6

1 (14-ounce) block organic extra-firm tofu

4 to 6 tablespoons extra virgin olive oil

3 cloves garlic, sliced or minced

1 yellow onion, diced

1/2 cup halved cherry tomatoes

2 cups fresh spinach

1 cup sliced fresh white button or cremini mushrooms

2 tablespoons onion powder

2 tablespoons garlic powder

2 tablespoons fresh or dried parsley

1/2 teaspoon turmeric

Salt and pepper, to taste

Vegan cheddar or mozzarella shreds, optional

Vegan bacon bits, optional

Buttered toast

Rinse the tofu and squeeze as much moisture out of it as you can. You can use paper towels to drain the excess liquid.

In a large skillet over medium heat, add the oil, garlic, and onion. Sauté until the garlic and onion become translucent, about 5 minutes.

Mash the tofu with your hands and add to the garlic and onion mixture in the skillet along with the tomatoes, spinach, and mushrooms. Stir in the onion powder, garlic powder, parsley, turmeric, and salt and pepper. At this point it will feel like you're making scrambled eggs!

Cook until spinach becomes slightly wilted and the tofu scramble is warm to your liking. Taste and adjust seasonings. Top with cheddar shreds and bacon bits, if using. Serve with buttered toast and juice, tea, or your fave cup of joe!

KID HELP

- Have your child squeeze out the excess liquid from the tofu over the sink.
- If old enough to use a knife, allow them to prep the vegetables that need cutting, like the tomatoes and mushrooms.
- When the scramble is done, let them top it with vegan bacon bits or have them butter their own toast. Everyone loves toast!

HOMEMADE FROSTED STRAWBERRY VEGAN TOASTER PASTRIES

Now this is what fun is made of! With the super easy vegan puff pastry crust, the strawberry center, and the frosting, you will be busting out sweet dance moves like nobody's watching.

Serves 6

Pastry

1 cup all-purpose flour

1/4 teaspoon pink Himalayan rock salt

5 ounces very cold vegan butter, cubed (I use Earth's Balance whipped vegan butter)

1/3 cup ice cold water

Filling

6 tablespoons strawberry jam, jelly, or preserves

Almond milk or water, as needed

Frosting

1 cup organic powdered sugar

1/2 teaspoon vanilla extract

2 tablespoons almond or coconut milk

Sprinkles, optional

Pastry

In a large bowl, mix together the flour and salt.

Add the butter and cut into flour mixture using a fork, 2 knives, or a pastry blender. It will have a super crumbly consistency and you want the butter to be no bigger than the size of a pea.

Make a well in the middle of the dough and pour in the water. Use your fork to mix and combine the dough until it starts to hold together.

Flour your work surface and rolling pin, and roll the dough into a 10-inch rectangle. It doesn't have to be perfect. Fold the dough into thirds by bringing the bottom part of the dough up to the middle of the dough and folding the upper part of the dough over the middle. You are going to repeat the rolling and folding process 8 times, rotating the dough a quarter of a turn each time before rolling out into a rectangle. Use flour as needed to prevent it from sticking to the work surface.

When you are done with the rolling and folding process, wrap the dough in plastic wrap and chill for 1 hour or overnight. I always get this prepped a day in advance when I know I'm making oven tarts.

When ready to use, roll out dough into an 8 x 9-inch rectangle. Cut in half lengthwise to form 2 (4 x 9-inch)

continued...

rectangles. Then cut each rectangle into thirds to create 3 (3 x 4-inch) rectangular pieces. All together you will have 12 even rectangle pieces, making 6 whole toaster pastries.

Preheat oven to 350 degrees.

Filling

Drop 1 tablespoon of jam in the middle of each of 6 dough rectangles. Using your fingers, moisten the edges with a little bit of almond milk or water and cover each with one of the remaining rectangles. Use a fork to press edges together to seal.

Poke the top of each toaster pastry 3 times with a fork. Brush tops with additional almond milk or water. Bake for 20 minutes, or until edges are golden. Remove from oven and let cool 5 minutes before transferring to a wire rack.

Frosting

Combine the sugar, vanilla, and milk together in a small bowl until smooth and creamy. If you want the frosting thicker, add more powdered sugar, if you'd like it runnier, add more milk, a tablespoon at a time.

Drizzle frosting over warm pastries and top with sprinkles, if desired. Serve right away or store in an airtight container in the refrigerator. To reheat, place in a 250 degree oven for 10–15 minutes.

KID HELP

- These pastries are so much fun to make with the kids. When you're done preparing the dough, let them knead it a few times or fold it over with you.
- Have them fill each pastry with the strawberry jam.
- And last but not least, (my favorite part) let them drizzle the icing and sprinkles on top!

STUFFED TORTILLA CHEESECAKE FRENCH TOAST

This is the best breakfast, dessert, or snack ever! Stuffed with healthy dark chocolate, strawberries, bananas, and vegan cream cheese, you legit can't go wrong.

Serves 6

6 ounces vegan cream cheese, room temperature

3 tablespoons maple syrup

1 tablespoon lemon juice

2 teaspoons vanilla extract

6 (8-inch) flour tortillas

6 large strawberries, sliced

2 bananas, sliced

1/2 bar vegan dark chocolate or 1/2 cup vegan chocolate chips

Whipped vegan butter, as needed

1/4 cup almond milk

2 flax eggs (page 23)

Coconut sugar, to sprinkle

In a large bowl whip together the cream cheese, syrup, lemon juice, and vanilla until combined. Spread 1 tablespoon (or more) of the cream cheese filling evenly over each tortilla. Place strawberry and banana slices over the cream cheese and top with chocolate pieces.

Roll tortillas tightly, starting with the edge closest to you until closed. The cream cheese will keep them together.

Melt some butter in a skillet over medium heat. Mix milk with the flax eggs. Working with 2 stuffed tortillas at a time, roll each in the egg wash then place in the hot skillet. Cook on each side for 3 minutes, or until golden brown. Repeat process with remaining stuffed tortillas.

To serve, sprinkle with coconut sugar and top with any remaining cream cheese filling, syrup, strawberries, or chocolate. Enjoy!

Note: You can prep the stuffed tortillas the night before to have them ready for breakfast. Just be sure to wrap them individually in plastic wrap to keep them from sticking together. You can also substitute the vegan cream cheese with Coconut Whipped Cream (page 196), and the almond milk with coconut milk or milk of choice.

continued...

Store cooked tortilla French toasts in an airtight container in the refrigerator for up to 3 days. This will give them that flakey, pastry-like texture. Once cooked they don't need to be individually wrapped as they won't stick together.

KID HELP

- Are you ready to get a little messy? When you have the egg wash ready, let your child roll each tortilla into it. Then they hand it to you so you can start the cooking process. It's fun to do this as a team.
- When the tortillas are done cooking and are cool to touch, let them sprinkle on the coconut sugar.
- Have your kid place the strawberries and extra cream cheese on top.
- Always have your kids help set the table or counter, and help with cleanup.

SUPER CHOCOLATEY EASY BROWNIE BREAKFAST BAKE

Yes, you can have brownies for breakfast! Loaded with chocolatey goodness, this bake is high in antioxidants to fight off those free radicals.

Serves 2

- ²/₃ cup gluten-free rolled oats
- 4 tablespoons brown rice flour
- 3 tablespoons cacao powder
- 1 teaspoon baking powder
- Pinch of salt
- ²/₃ cup almond milk, plus extra
- 2 to 3 tablespoons maple syrup
- 2 teaspoons coconut oil, melted
- 1 teaspoon vanilla extract
- 3 tablespoons carob chips or dairy-free chocolate chips, plus extra

Preheat oven to 325 degrees. Prepare 2 ramekins with coconut oil spray or nonstick cooking spray.

In a medium bowl, whisk together oats, flour, cacao powder, baking powder, and salt. Add the milk, syrup, oil, and vanilla and mix until combined well. Fold in carob chips. Divide the batter evenly among the ramekins and bake for 15–20 minutes.

Remove from oven and let cool for a few minutes. To serve, top with extra carob chips and a splash of almond milk, if desired. Enjoy!

KID HELP

- Once you have all the ingredients in a bowl, let your child do the mixing as best they can. When they're done, if you need to, give it a once over to make sure it's well-combined.
- When ramekins are cool to touch after baking, let the kids top with extra chocolate chips or cacao nibs. Kids love that extra melty chocolate.
- Have them help with cleanup when breakfast is over.

STRAWBERRIES AND CREAM WARM OATS

One of my fave combos, this dream of a dish serves up sexy strawberries that provide an awesome amount of vitamin C. Paired with the dairy free yogurt; your gut will be doing a happy dance for sure.

Serves 2

2 cups coconut milk

1 cup rolled oats

Pinch of salt

4 tablespoons maple syrup

6 fresh strawberries, chopped, plus extra

2 teaspoons vanilla extract

$1/2$ cup dairy-free yogurt

$1/2$ cup strawberry jam

In a medium saucepan over medium heat, bring the milk to a boil. Turn heat down and add the oats, salt, syrup, and strawberries. Cook for 5 minutes until oats are soft and tender. Remove from heat and stir in vanilla.

Divide into 2 bowls. Spoon the yogurt and jam into 2 separate ziplock bags and twist to squeeze the air out of each bag to force contents into one of the corners. Cut the tip off the corner of the yogurt bag to create a small hole. Squeeze half of the yogurt into one of the bowls over the oats in a spiral design. Repeat process with the jam. You may need to make a larger hole in the corner if your jam has strawberry chunks. Repeat with second bowl and remaining yogurt and jam.

Note: You can adjust sweetness to your liking with more or less maple syrup.

KID HELP

- Have your kids set the table for breakfast. I like to give my son the plates, napkins, spoons, cups, and the breakfast beverage of choice.
- Let them swirl the jam and yogurt on top of their oats. Alternatively, you can just let them scoop the jam and yogurt out in true kid fashion and do as they please with the topping.

BROCCOLI AND QUINOA BREAKFAST PATTIES

Made with broccoli, quinoa, carrots, and flax seeds, this is truly a healthy addition to your morning routine. It is sure to hit a home run with the fam.

Makes approximately 10 patties

1 cup uncooked quinoa

2 cups low sodium vegetable broth

$1/2$ cube vegetable bouillon, optional

1 cup shredded broccoli and carrot mixture

2 flax eggs (page 23)

$1/2$ cup gluten-free breadcrumbs

2 cloves garlic, minced

$1^1/2$ teaspoons garlic powder

$1^1/2$ teaspoons onion powder

2 teaspoons fresh or dried parsley

2 tablespoons coconut oil or extra virgin olive oil, plus extra for cooking

Salt and pepper, to taste

Vegan Sour Cream (page 184)

Chopped fresh parsley, optional

Green onions, sliced, optional

Rinse quinoa thoroughly and place in a saucepan with vegetable broth and vegetable bouillon, if using. Bring to a boil, reduce heat, and let simmer for 15 minutes. The quinoa will absorb all the broth.

In a large bowl, add cooked quinoa, broccoli mixture, flax eggs, breadcrumbs, garlic, garlic powder, onion powder, parsley, 2 tablespoons oil, and salt and pepper; mix well to combine.

Drizzle a little oil into a skillet over medium heat. Make palm-size balls out of the mixture. Place in skillet and flatten with a spatula. Cook on both sides for 2–3 minutes, or until crisp and golden brown. Place patties on a plate lined with a paper towel to drain. Serve warm with sour cream, parsley, and onions.

Store leftovers in an airtight container in the refrigerator for up to 5 days, maybe a little longer. Enjoy!

 **KID HELP**

- Let your kids make the balls out of the mixture. This will give them a direct hands-on experience.
- Have your kids top the patties with sour cream and onions.
- Let your kids be the taste testers.

APPLE CINNAMON CREPES

Apples are super rich in fiber, aiding in a healthy stomach, and these delicious crepes are like having warm apple pie for breakfast, but with better ingredients.

Makes 12 crepes

Crepes

1 cup plus 1 tablespoon all-purpose flour

$1\frac{1}{2}$ cups almond milk

1 mashed banana

2 flax eggs (page 23)

1 teaspoon vanilla extract

Apple Filling

2 Granny Smith apples, sliced, plus extra for garnish

$\frac{1}{4}$ cup organic brown or coconut sugar

$\frac{1}{4}$ cup water

2 teaspoons cinnamon

$\frac{1}{4}$ teaspoon nutmeg

1 teaspoon vegan butter

$\frac{1}{2}$ teaspoon apple cider vinegar

Coconut Whipped Cream (page 196), to top

Crepes

In a large bowl, mix crepe ingredients together until well-combined. The batter should be super runny.

Heat a large nonstick skillet and pour $\frac{1}{3}$ cup batter into the center. Swirl the batter around to completely coat the bottom. When the edges start to turn up, lift the crepe up a little bit and check to see if it is browned. If so, flip the crepe and let it cook until slightly crispy. Remove from pan to a plate and cover each crepe with a damp paper towel to keep them moist.

Filling

Place all the filling ingredients, except whipped cream and extra apples in a large skillet over medium heat; mix until combined. Sauté for 10 minute, or until sugar is dissolved and the liquid in the pan starts to thicken. Once apples are soft and browned a bit and the liquid is thick, you're ready to assemble the crepes.

Spread some of the apple mixture over one side of each crepe. Top apples with a little bit of the caramel sauce from the pan. Fold the crepe in half over the apples then fold in half again making a triangle. Top with whipped cream, caramel drizzle, and extra apple slices to serve.

KID HELP

- When the crepes are done cooking, have your child fill each one with the apple filling.
- Let everyone top their own crepes.

QUINOA PORRIDGE WITH BLUEBERRY SAUCE

Quinoa is often thought to be a grain, but it's really a seed! This powerful, protein-filled seed is not meant for only lunch and dinner; it's great for breakfast porridges, too! It provides a good kick of energy that won't have you crashing come noon.

Serves 2

- 2 cups almond milk
- 1 cup uncooked tricolor quinoa
- 1 tablespoon maple syrup, plus extra
- 1 teaspoon vanilla extract
- 1/3 cup blueberries, plus extra
- 2 tablespoons water
- 1 banana, sliced, optional
- 1/4 cup coconut milk yogurt or any dairy-free yogurt, optional

In a medium saucepan, bring almond milk and quinoa to a boil; cover and simmer for 15 minutes until liquid is absorbed. Add 1 tablespoon maple syrup and vanilla; mix well.

While the quinoa is cooking, prepare the blueberry sauce by adding the blueberries and water to a small saucepan. Cook on medium heat, pressing down with a spatula to make some of the blueberries burst, until hot and syrupy. Remove from heat and let the sauce cool.

Once quinoa is ready, divide between 2 bowls. Top with blueberry sauce, banana slices, extra blueberries, a drizzle of maple syrup, and yogurt.

KID HELP

- Have your kid rinse the blueberries, if using fresh. They can snack on them while they wait for breakfast to be ready.
- Have them prepare the banana slices.
- When the quinoa is divided in the bowls, let them top their porridge with suggested toppings.

LEMON-COCONUT MUFFINS

These quick and easy muffins have the perfect lemon-to-coconut ratio, come packed with nutrients, and are loaded with flavor. They're great for breakfast or as a snack on the go.

Makes 12 muffins

$1/4$ cup vegan butter, softened to room temperature

$1/2$ cup organic sugar

1 flax egg (page 23) or $1/4$ cup applesauce

1 teaspoon vanilla extract

1 teaspoon coconut extract

Zest of 1 lemon

2 tablespoons lemon juice

1 cup organic all-purpose flour or whole wheat flour

$1 1/2$ teaspoons baking powder

$1/2$ cup shredded coconut, plus extra

$1/2$ cup vegan plain yogurt

Preheat oven to 350 degrees. Prepare a standard muffin pan with nonstick cooking spray.

In a large bowl, mix together the butter and sugar until creamy. Add the flax egg or applesauce, both extracts, and lemon zest and juice. Mix well.

In a small bowl, combine the flour, baking powder, and coconut. Stir into the butter mixture. Add the yogurt and mix until no streaks remain.

Fill the muffin cups about $2/3$ full with batter and sprinkle the tops with extra shredded coconut. Bake for 30–35 minutes, or until muffins are golden brown on top. Store in an airtight container for up to 1 week.

KID HELP

- Direct your kids on how to add either the wet or dry ingredients to a bowl.
- When everything is in one bowl, let them do the mixing the best they can. Once they're done, give it a good whisk or use a hand mixer to make sure it's mixed well.
- Give them a scoop and have them fill the muffin cups with the batter.

VEGAN BUTTERMILK PANCAKES

These are the most awesomest vegan pancakes ever! This will be your go-to recipe to serve up hot, fluffy pancakes with a side of deliciousness each time.

Serves 4 to 6

2 flax eggs (page 23)

2 cups coconut milk

1 tablespoon apple cider vinegar

2 cups all-purpose flour

2 teaspoons baking powder

1 teaspoon baking soda

2 tablespoons organic sugar or monk fruit sweetener

Pinch of salt

1 teaspoon vanilla extract

$1/2$ teaspoon vegan butter

Mixed berries

Maple syrup

Powdered sugar

Prep the flax eggs and put them in the refrigerator to thicken up for 5 minutes. In a small bowl, mix the coconut milk and vinegar together and let set for 5 minutes. This makes vegan buttermilk.

In a large bowl, whisk together the flour, baking powder, baking soda, sugar, and salt. Add the flax eggs and vanilla to the vegan buttermilk and whisk to combine.

Pour the wet ingredients into the dry ingredients and mix well using a fork. Do not over mix; it is okay if there are small lumps left in the batter.

Heat a large skillet or griddle over medium heat and melt the butter. Pour $1/2$ cup of the batter onto the skillet and cook both sides of the pancake until golden brown. Serve with mixed berries, maple syrup, and a shake of powdered sugar.

KID HELP

- Have your child measure out the dry or wet ingredients while you do the other.
- Let them mix the batter, and you can totally taste it because it's vegan.
- When the pancakes are done, let your child help top with berries or sprinkle with powdered sugar.

KID-FRIENDLY SHAKES

"ROYALTY OF ALL DRINKS"

Healthy shakes and smoothies are not just an awesome trend (that won't ever go out of style); they are like the royalty of all drinks! When made right, they provide sufficient amounts of nutrients that our bodies require, and kids absolutely love them, even if they have veggies tucked away inside. These shakes are my go-to recipes for everyday health for both me and for my family.

THE VEGGIE SHAKE

Kale is loaded with fiber and nutrients like potassium, vitamin C, and vitamin B6 that support the heart, and when blended in shakes it's easily digested.

The natural sweetness of the grapes and banana help disguise the sometimes bitter taste kale can have.

Serves 1

$1/2$ cup kale

1 avocado

$1/4$ cup red grapes

1 fresh or frozen banana

1 cup water, coconut water, or almond milk

Ice, as desired

Place all ingredients into a high-speed blender and blend until smooth.

KID HELP

- Have your child rinse off any fruit and veggies that need cleaning.
- Have them help you get all ingredients into the blender.
- Let your child pick out their favorite cup with a straw!

THE HULK SHAKE

Spinach is that dark leafy green veggie we all should be eating. It is good for hair, skin, nails, and bone health.

High in protein, folate, iron, and all the important minerals, this is one veggie you don't want to pass up!

Serves 1

1 cup spinach

1 cup almond milk or water

1 tablespoon flax seeds or chia seeds

$1/2$ cup fresh or canned pineapple chunks

1 tablespoon almond butter

1 fresh or frozen banana

Ice, as desired

Place all ingredients into a high-speed blender and blend until smooth.

KID HELP

- Let your child help get all the ingredients gathered.
- Have them add the pineapple and ice to the blender.
- Let them turn the blender on (make sure the lid is on and secure) and watch how excited they get to see their shake being made!

MICHAEL'S STRAWBERRY SHAKE

Good for the brain, eyes, and heart, strawberries are known for their high content of antioxidants and vitamin C! This berry is a powerhouse of a super-food. They are naturally sweet, come packed with a huge nutritional punch, and kids LOVE them. Way to go strawberries!

Serves 1

5 fresh strawberries or $^1/_2$ cup frozen strawberries

1 fresh or frozen banana

1 cup dairy-free milk, of choice

Ice, as desired

Place all ingredients into a high-speed blender and blend until smooth.

KID HELP

- Have your child clean the strawberries.
- Have them add all ingredients to the blender.
- Let them turn on the blender (make sure the lid is on securely).

PEACHY PIÑA COLADA SHAKE

Pineapples are super sweet all on their own, but don't let their sweetness fool you. This gorgeous yellow stunner has an enzyme in it called bromelain. It fights inflammation along with its anti-bacterial properties and can help with coughs by soothing and calming the airways.

Serves 1

1 fresh or frozen banana

1/2 cup fresh pineapple chunks

1 fresh peach or 1/2 cup frozen peaches

1 cup coconut milk

1 teaspoon coconut essence or extract

Ice, as desired

Place all ingredients into a high-speed blender and blend until smooth.

KID HELP

- Have your child gather all the fruit needed.
- Let them add all ingredients to the blender.
- If old enough, let them pour the shake into their favorite smoothie jar with a straw, and have them top it with some extra fruit!

THE COCO LOCO SHAKE

Need an immunity boost? Coconut kills off viruses, fungi, bacteria, and even parasites. Loaded with healthy fats, potassium, magnesium, and electrolytes, this gem will consistently provide you with nutrients to maintain optimal health.

Serves 1

1 cup coconut milk

1 fresh or frozen banana

2 dates, pits removed

1/2 cup frozen coconut meat, optional

1 teaspoon cinnamon

1/4 cup water or more as needed

Ice, as desired

Place all ingredients into a high-speed blender and blend until smooth.

KID HELP

- Let your child help you get all the ingredients.
- Have your child get any toppings they may want ready.
- Let them add ingredients to the blender and run it (be sure the lid is secure).

THE RAZZ SHAKE

Raspberries are a great mood and memory enhancer, and help regulate heartbeat and blood pressure.

They are super high in vitamin C and other essential vitamins and minerals.

Serves 1

¹/₂ cup fresh or frozen raspberries

1 fresh or frozen banana

1 tablespoon peanut butter or almond butter

1 cup unsweetened almond milk

Ice, as desired

Place all ingredients into a high-speed blender and blend until smooth.

 **KID HELP**

- Have your child rinse the raspberries.
- Let them dollop the peanut butter or almond butter into the blender then have them lick the spoon!
- If old enough, let them pour the shake into their favorite jar and top with more raspberries.

BLUEBERRY SHAKE

Blueberries are natural healers. They help cleanse the blood and liver and provide many essential vitamins and minerals. Known for their high levels of antioxidants, this is one berry you don't want to skip out on. Great for eye and gum health, too!

Serves 1

1 cup fresh or frozen blueberries

1 fresh or frozen banana

1 pitted Medjool date

1/2 large zucchini, cut into chunks

1 cup almond milk

Ice, as desired

Place all ingredients into a high-speed blender and blend until smooth.

KID HELP

- Have your child clean and rinse the blueberries.
- Once you have everything ready to go, let your child add it all to the blender.
- Get some cleanup help that is age appropriate.

THE TROPICAL SHAKE

Mangoes are one of the sweetest fruits out there and I love them. They're loaded with goodness like beta-carotene, which is a must for our immune system. They also delay aging, cure acne, and so much more!

Serves 1

1 fresh or frozen banana

1 cup fresh or frozen mango chunks

1 cup apple juice

$^1/_4$ teaspoon turmeric powder

$^1/_2$ cup almond milk

Ice, as desired

Place all ingredients into a high-speed blender and blend until smooth.

KID HELP

- Have your child help you add all of the ingredients to the blender.
- Have them turn it on so they can watch their creation being made. Be sure the lid is on nice and secure.

MOTHER OF DRAGONS SHAKE

Pitaya, also known as dragon fruit, is loaded with antioxidants, fiber, calcium, phosphorus, iron, and niacin. It has extremely high amounts of vitamin C, B1, B2, and B3. It's also one of the only fruits where you eat the seeds. The seeds contain healthy fats and protein, and that makes this fruit even more unique.

Serves 1

1 (3.5-ounce) package frozen pitaya (dragon fruit)

$1/2$ cup fresh or frozen pineapple chunks

2 tablespoons coconut sugar

1 cup almond milk

1 fresh or frozen banana

Ice, as desired

1 handful shredded coconut, optional

Place all ingredients except shredded coconut into a high-speed blender and blend until smooth. Sprinkle with coconut, if desired.

KID HELP

- Have your child add the pitaya to the blender.
- Have them turn on the blender so they can watch their creation being made. Be sure the lid is on nice and secure. Kids are always in awe of this shake's color because it is hot pink.
- You can turn this shake into a smoothie bowl and have you child top the bowl with their fave toppings—coconut shavings, extra pineapple chunks, chia seeds, or dairy free chocolate chips!

ORANGE CREAMSICLE

We all know oranges are one of the leading sources of vitamin C, but they also can help lower cholesterol, are high in potassium, and boost heart health.

Serves 1

¹/₂ cup coconut milk or almond milk

¹/₄ cup plain or vanilla dairy-free yogurt

1 teaspoon vanilla extract

1 large orange, peeled

1 fresh or frozen banana

Ice, as desired

Pinch of turmeric powder, optional

Orange slices, optional

Coconut Whipped Cream (page 196), optional

Place coconut milk, yogurt, vanilla, orange, banana, ice, and turmeric into a high-speed blender and blend until smooth and creamy. Garnish glasses with orange slices and top with Coconut Whipped Cream. Serve and enjoy.

 **KID HELP**

- Have your child peel the orange.
- Let them add all ingredients to the blender.
- Show them how the turmeric will change the color.
- Let them garnish their glasses with orange slices that they can totally eat!

LUNCHES

"NO ONE LIKES A BORING LUNCH"

We all have busy days that are often both so mentally and physically demanding that sometimes we forget to have a good lunch. Lunch is just as important as breakfast. It has to carry us through until dinner.

And, think about how taxing school is for our kids. They need to be able to focus. They're functioning on every level and using so much energy thinking and learning. Lunch plays a huge role in the nutrition intake our kids get in their day. They need a balanced lunch to keep them full, but also a lunch that tastes good and that they look forward to. No one likes a boring lunch, especially our kids, so here you'll find easy-to-make lunches that are full of nourishment and are packed with taste, texture, and fun!

CARROTS IN A BLANKET

No little piggies were harmed in the making of these blankets! They are the perfect veggie appetizer or lunch for kids and adults alike. Dip into classic yellow mustard and enjoy the flakiness of the puff pastry and sweetness of the carrot.

Makes 12 carrots in a blanket

12 whole baby carrots

1 tablespoon coconut oil or olive oil

Salt and pepper, to taste

1 generous tablespoon dried dill weed

1 package vegan puff pastry* thawed or homemade (see page 36)

Yellow mustard, for dipping

* If using a store-bought puff pastry be sure to read the label to confirm it's vegan.

Preheat oven to 350 degrees. Line a baking sheet with parchment paper.

In a saucepan, cover carrots in water and boil until just tender. Do not let them get super soft or they will break. Remove from water and let cool for 5 minutes.

In a skillet, heat the oil. Add in carrots, salt, pepper, and dill; toss to coat. Cook, stirring until extra golden, 5–6 minutes.

Roll out pastry, and cut into 12 rectangular pieces just wide enough to wrap around carrots, leaving both ends exposed. The carrots should be about 2 inches long.

Wrap a piece of pastry around each carrot and lightly brush edges with water; pinch to seal closed. Lay wrapped carrots, seam side down, on baking sheet.

Bake for 15–20 minutes, or until pastry puffs are golden and crisp. Remove from oven and let cool 5 minutes before serving, if you can wait! Serve with mustard.

KID HELP

- Let your child help roll out the dough. Give them just a small piece so they can mimic what you're doing.
- Let your child wrap the carrots in the puff pastry.
- Have them brush the edges with water and pinch them closed.

PASTA SALAD WITH VEGAN MAYO

This fun pasta salad is perfect as a side dish, a main course, or to take to a BBQ.

Serves 4 to 6

1 pound dry pasta, of choice*

2 tablespoons extra virgin olive oil

1 cup vegan mayonnaise

1/2 yellow onion, diced, optional

1 (15-ounce) can peas, drained

Salt and pepper, to taste

* I suggest using a regular pasta. Sometimes rice, quinoa, or other types of non-wheat pasta don't hold up very well in this dish.

Cook pasta according to package instructions. Drain and place in a serving bowl. Add the oil and toss to coat so the pasta doesn't stick together; let cool for 10 minutes.

Once the pasta has cooled a bit, add the mayonnaise, onion, if using and peas. Season with salt and pepper, and mix well.

Serve right away or keep in the refrigerator. It is great warm or cold, and is tasty even a few days later!

Tip: Canned peas do not have to be cooked before using them in this dish. If you are using frozen peas, let them thaw to room temperature, or lightly steam them, before adding to the pasta.

 **KID HELP**

- Have your child add in the mayo and peas, and if they want, the onion, too.
- Have them mix the pasta as best they can then you can add the seasonings and let them do a taste test.

VEGGIE PINWHEELS

My son loves to help me make these fun pinwheels. He eats the veggies while we're rolling. And then we have a rockin' good lunch!

Makes 16 pinwheels

2 (8-inch) flour tortillas

4 tablespoons vegan cream cheese, divided

$1/2$ cup fresh spinach, divided

4 to 8 slices red, yellow, or orange bell pepper, divided

Spread 2 tablespoons cream cheese on each tortilla.

Arrange $1/4$ cup spinach and 2 to 4 slices of bell pepper on top of the cream cheese on each tortilla. Roll up tortillas and cut into 1-inch-thick pinwheels.

KID HELP

- Let your child taste test the veggies.
- Have them spread the cream cheese across the tortillas and let them arrange the veggies.
- Let them do the rolling then you can tighten it up if need be before cutting into pinwheels.

VEGGIE AND BEAN RICE BOWLS

This is a super easy meal to put together. The only cooking required is for the rice. You can make the rice ahead of time so you have it ready when you need it. The fun part is you can let your family fix their own bowls with whatever toppings they want!

Serves 2

2 cups cooked white jasmine or basmati rice, divided

2 tomatoes, diced

1 avocado, diced

1 white onion, diced

$1/4$ cup sliced black olives

Handful of vegan cheese shreds, of choice

$1/4$ cup cooked or canned black beans, drained and rinsed

Salt and pepper, to taste

1 lime, sliced in wedges

Handful of fresh cilantro, optional

Place 1 cup of rice in each bowl and top each with tomatoes, avocado, onion, olives, cheese, beans salt, pepper, and cilantro to taste. Serve right away and enjoy.

KID HELP

- Let your child help you prepare by putting the olives, tomatoes, and beans in separate bowls. This makes it easier when it comes time to add the toppings.
- Have them rinse the cilantro.
- Let your kids create their own rice bowls. The more veggies the better!

VEGAN PHILLY CHEESESTEAK

Eating vegan does not mean giving up all that you love. You can still enjoy your favorite foods, but with better, healthier ingredients. In this recipe the "cheese" is made with almond milk and some spices to give you this classic, fun meal!

Serves 6

Steak

1 container (about 4 cups) organic seitan,* sliced into thin pieces

3 tablespoons extra virgin olive oil

¼ cup Bragg Liquid Aminos or organic soy sauce

1 (16-ounce) bag frozen bell peppers and onions

Cheese Sauce

1 cup unsweetened almond milk

1½ tablespoons extra virgin olive oil

¼ cup all-purpose flour

1 teaspoon yellow mustard

¼ teaspoon turmeric powder, optional

1½ cups water

¼ cup Bragg Liquid Aminos or organic soy sauce

1 cup nutritional yeast

Salt and pepper, to taste

Side salad, fries, or fresh spinach leaves, optional

6 deli sandwich rolls

Steak

Preheat oven to 375 degrees. Line a baking sheet with parchment paper.

Place the seitan slices on the baking sheet and coat evenly with oil and liquid aminos. Bake for 10 minutes.

While the seitan is baking, prepare the peppers and onions. You can use fresh bell peppers and onions, but I find it saves a lot of time to use frozen. Steam the frozen vegetables for 12 minutes, until tender but not overdone.

Combine steak and vegetables in a bowl; set aside.

Cheese Sauce

In a saucepan over medium heat, whisk together the milk, oil, flour, mustard, and turmeric until smooth.

Add the water, liquid aminos, and nutritional yeast; cook for 10 minutes, whisking frequently until it starts to thicken. Season with salt and pepper. If sauce seems too runny, add 1 tablespoon flour, but keep in mind that it will thicken as it cools.

To Assemble

Pour some of the cheese sauce into the steak mixture; toss to coat.

Slice the rolls in half lengthwise and fill with the steak mixture. Spoon desired amount of cheese sauce over the filling and serve with a side salad or fries. You can add some fresh spinach if you'd like, too.

* Seitan is a textured wheat protein that acts as a good meat substitution for special occasions.

KID HELP

- Show your child the seitan and explain to them what it is. Show them how you cook it.
- Have your child set the table and get the sandwich rolls ready.
- Let them mix the cheese sauce when it's done cooking.
- Have them fix their own sandwich. Typically everyone reaches for more of the cheese sauce. And I don't blame them, it's delicious!

CHICKPEA SALAD SANDWICH

Chickpeas are a great sub to just about anything as they're a go-to source for plant-based protein and fiber. Just what you need in the afternoon to keep your energy up and your belly full.

Makes 2 to 3 sandwiches

1 (15-ounce) can chickpeas or garbanzo beans, drained and rinsed

$3/4$ cup vegan mayonnaise

2 tablespoons extra virgin olive oil

1 cup halved red grapes

$1/2$ tablespoon dried dill weed

Salt and pepper, to taste

$1/2$ to $3/4$ cup baby kale

4 to 6 slices bread of choice, toasted

Side salad or fruit, optional

In a bowl, mash the chickpeas so that there aren't any whole pieces left. Add the mayonnaise, oil, grapes, dill, salt and pepper. Mix well.

Spread filling evenly over half the bread slices and top each with $1/4$ cup kale. Place remaining slices of bread over top and serve with a side salad or fresh fruit.

KID HELP

- When you rinse and drain the chickpeas, let your kid smash them up with a masher or fork.
- Have them add in the mayo and seasonings and give it a mix.
- Assemble the sandwiches together as a team because it's more fun that way!

VEGGIE CHEESE QUESADILLAS

Who says you can't have your quesadilla and eat it too? Not this gal! Don't be alarmed—these are the healthy version of the oh-so-bad-for-you fast food. It's ok if right about now you want to do a little dance, make a little love, and pretty much get down tonight.

Serves 2

2 (10-inch) flour tortillas

1 avocado, sliced

1 tomato, diced (you might not use all of it)

2 slices vegan cheese, of choice

1 tablespoon Vegan Sour Cream (page 184), plus extra

1 handful fresh cilantro, optional

Salt and pepper, to taste

Limes, to garnish

Take 1 tortilla and spread avocado slices across it. Top with tomato, cheese, sour cream, and cilantro; season with salt and pepper. Place second tortilla directly on top.

Heat a large skillet and lightly spray with olive oil cooking spray.

Place the stuffed quesadilla in the skillet and cook for 5 minutes on each side, or until golden brown and crispy. Be careful when flipping the quesadilla so the filling doesn't fall out.

Remove from skillet, and use a pizza cutter or large knife to cut into quarters. Top with sour cream, cilantro, and a sprinkle of lime juice.

KID HELP

- As if in a cooking class, let your kids follow you step-by-step when assembling the quesadilla.
- You do the cooking and cutting and let them do their own dollop of sour cream and a squeeze of lime.

TOASTED AVOCADO AND BEAN PITAS

This takes avocado toast to a whole new level. Loaded with plant-based protein and healthy fats, this is just another way lunch is served up right, vegan style!

Serves 4

4 whole-wheat vegan pitas

1 (15-ounce) can red kidney beans, drained and rinsed

2 teaspoons garlic powder, divided

Salt and pepper, to taste

4 ripe avocados

4 tablespoons Vegan Sour Cream (page 184), divided

2 green onions or scallions, sliced

Preheat oven to 325 degrees. Line a baking sheet with parchment paper.

Place pitas on baking sheet and warm in oven for about 10 minutes. Remember, you don't want them too crispy, unless you prefer them that way.

While the pitas are toasting in the oven, place beans in a small skillet over medium heat. Season with salt and pepper and 1 teaspoon garlic powder. Cook until heated through, 5–6 minutes.

Mash the avocados and add salt, pepper, and remaining garlic powder; mix well.

To assemble, spread a generous spoonful of mashed avocado across a warm pita. Sprinkle $\frac{1}{4}$ to $\frac{1}{3}$ cup beans over the avocado and 1 tablespoon of sour cream. Top with onions and season with salt and pepper.

Note: You can substitute any bean of choice, and replace the sour cream with hummus.

KID HELP

- Give your kids the avocados and let them mash them up while the pitas are toasting.
- Let them assemble their own pitas while you're assembling yours.

AVOCADO AND HUMMUS MINI QUESADILLAS

Who's in the mood for a quesadilla?! If you answered yes then you've come to the right place. (Five second dance party, haaay!) Ok, but seriously, avocado and hummus pressed together, warm with melted cheese! Aah-mazing!

Makes 8 mini quesadillas

2 (10-inch) flour tortillas

2 to 3 tablespoons hummus

1 avocado, sliced into 8 slices

Vegan cheese shreds, of choice, to taste

Salt and pepper, to taste

The Best Vegan Cheese Wiz (page 193), optional

Vegan Sour Cream (page 184), optional

Use a 2^1/$_2$-inch round cookie cutter to cut 4 mini tortillas out of each tortilla. If you don't have a cookie cutter, use the top of a glass cup.

Spread hummus on one side of each mini tortilla, and top with a slice of avocado, a sprinkle of cheese, and salt and pepper. Fold the tortillas in half.

Spray a skillet with nonstick cooking spray and heat over medium heat. Cook each mini tortilla on both sides, until golden brown. Serve with cheese sauce and sour cream for dipping.

Note: If mini tortillas are available at your grocery store, you can use them in this recipe to help get lunch on the table a little bit quicker.

KID HELP

- Let your kids help with making the mini tortillas. Give them the cookie cutter and let them have at it.
- Have them spread the hummus across their tortillas and add the avocado and cheese. Adults do the cooking.

BERRY GRILLED CHEESE

Loaded with anti-oxidants, this savory-yet-sweet sammie is perfect for any season. Melted cheese, berries, and spinach make this an ultimate winner!

Makes 2 sandwiches

1 cup blueberries

1 cup sliced strawberries

$1^1/_2$ tablespoons coconut sugar

1 tablespoon balsamic vinaigrette

4 slices bread, of choice

4 teaspoons vegan butter, divided

2 cups spinach, divided

1 cup vegan mozzarella cheese shreds, divided

Salt and pepper, to taste

In a saucepan on medium heat, mix together the blueberries, strawberries, sugar, and vinaigrette. Smash berries gently as you stir, and bring to a boil.

Remove berries from saucepan and place in a strainer over a bowl. You can use the leftover juice as a salad dressing.

Spread 1 side of each slice of bread with 1 teaspoon butter. Place 2 slices of bread, buttered side down in a large skillet that has been heated over medium heat. Divide the berry mixture in half and spread each half over the unbuttered side of the 2 slices of bread. Top with 1 cup spinach, $1/_2$ cup cheese, and salt and pepper. Replace the remaining 2 slices of bread, buttered side up, on the sandwiches and fry until golden brown on each side.

Note: Make more of the berry mixture than needed for topping the sandwich. A panini press would work great too.

KID HELP

- Let your child help rinse the berries.
- Before you put the berries on the stove, let them mash them up a bit for you.

CARROT DOGS

Plant-based veggie dogs are so much fun! Especially when things like this are super easy to make, not processed, and healthy for you. Watch out hot dogs, we have a new sheriff in town.

Serves 4

4 thick carrots

4 hot dog buns

Mustard

Ketchup

Relish

Toppings, of choice

Clean the carrots and cut off the tops and bottoms. If you want the carrot dogs to really look like traditional wieners, peel the carrots and cut, rounding the ends, to match the size of the bun. Bring a large pot of water to a boil. Place carrots into hot water and let cook until fork tender, about 20 minutes.

Remove carrots from the water and grill them, or leave as is. Serve with your favorite condiments and toppings, such as mustard, ketchup, and relish. You can even make a vegan chili and top them with that and sauerkraut.

See? So simple, easy, and completely delicious.

Note: Use whole-wheat organic hot dog buns for an added nutritional boost.

KID HELP

- Have your kids help with cleaning the carrots. Fresh carrots are so much fun to hold, and with their long green leaves, kids are in awe of them.
- Let them load up their own carrot dog with all the fixings.

SNACKS

"WE HAVE SNACKS FOR A REASON"

Having quality snack options is a game changer. Yes, we have breakfast, lunch, and dinner, but we also have snacks for a reason. Snacks help keep us from getting overly hungry and devouring everything in sight. Having ready-made snacks that we can pack for school or take on-the-go will help us steer clear of the processed junk that is all too easily accessible.

ROASTED CHICKPEAS

Hands down, this is one of my fave snacks. Not only are they great to add to things like salads, all on their own they provide a nice boost of energy because of their high protein content. And they taste amaze!

Makes about 2 cups

- 1 (15-ounce) can chickpeas (garbanzo beans)
- 2 tablespoons extra virgin olive oil
- 1 tablespoon onion powder
- 1 tablespoon garlic powder
- 1 tablespoon fresh or dried parsley
- Salt and pepper, to taste

Preheat oven to 350 degrees. Line a baking sheet with parchment paper.

Drain and rinse the chickpeas. Spread them out on the baking sheet. Using a paper towel, pat the chickpeas dry and roll around until mostly dry. It's ok if the skin comes off.

Drizzle with olive oil and sprinkle with onion powder, garlic powder, and parsley. Season with salt and pepper, and stir until evenly coated.

Bake for 25–30 minutes, stirring halfway through. Remove from oven and let cool for a few minutes before eating.

Serve right away and snack on! Store in the fridge in an airtight container or ziplock bag. They will lose their crunch and become soft but will still be amazingly delicious and snackable.

Note: The longer you bake the chickpeas, the crispier they become. Don't leave them in longer than 30 minutes unless you want them on the harder side.

 **KID HELP**

- Let your child pat the chickpeas dry and roll them around on the baking sheet.
- When you're finished adding the seasonings, have your child roll them around with a spoon or fork so they are evenly coated in the spices. There's no right or wrong way to do this.

HOMEMADE OVEN-BAKED TORTILLA CHIPS

I'm a sucker for chips. But I'd rather make my own because I know exactly what ingredients are being used. These chips are perfect on their own, for hummus dipping, or, if you want to be completely daring, top them with my vegan cheese sauce, and voilà . . . nachos!

Serves 2 to 4

5 (10-inch) flour tortillas

3 tablespoons extra virgin olive oil

1¹/₂ tablespoons onion powder

1¹/₂ tablespoons garlic powder

1¹/₂ tablespoons dried parsley

1¹/₂ tablespoons dried basil

1¹/₂ tablespoons dried oregano

Salt and pepper, to taste

Preheat oven to 350 degrees. Line a baking sheet with parchment paper.

Cut each tortilla into 8 wedges. Arrange tortillas on baking sheet without overlapping.

In a small bowl, combine the oil, onion powder, garlic powder, parsley, basil, and oregano.

Generously brush or rub the oil mixture over each tortilla and sprinkle with extra salt and pepper, if needed. Bake for 10–15 minutes, until lightly golden brown. Halfway through the baking time, flip the tortillas and lightly brush with the oil mixture.

Store in a container on the counter for up to a week.

KID HELP

- After you cut the tortillas into wedges, have your kid spread them out on the baking sheet.
- Have them either rub or brush the tortilla wedges with the oil. This doesn't have to be perfect.
- Season as instructed, and have your child set a timer.

SWEET POTATO MOUSSE

I can't even deal with how amazingly delicious this is. Who knew chocolate and sweet potatoes, right!? Not only do sweet potatoes provide a boatload of nutrients supporting the immune system and helping our organs work properly, these gems are naturally sweet all on their own. They truly live up to their name.

Serves 4

1 large sweet potato, baked, cooled, and peeled

1/2 cup full-fat coconut milk

6 pitted Medjool dates

1/2 cup cacao or cocoa powder

2 teaspoons vanilla extract

1 teaspoon cinnamon, plus extra

1/2 cup water, plus extra

4 tablespoons maple syrup, plus extra

Coconut Whipped Cream (page 196)

Place the sweet potato, milk, dates, cacao powder, vanilla, cinnamon, and maple syrup into a high-speed blender and blend until smooth and creamy.

If too thick, add more water, 1 tablespoon at a time, until you reach desired consistency. Adjust sweetness with additional maple syrup if desired.

Divide between individual serving dishes and top with Coconut Whipped Cream and a dash of cinnamon. Serve right away, or store in the fridge in an airtight container for up to 5 days.

 **KID HELP**

- Let your child peel away the skin from the sweet potato when cooled. It easily comes right off after baking.
- Throw all ingredients in the blender and let your child hit the on switch (with lid on securely).
- Serve it up in their fave bowl and let them top it with coconut whip and some dark chocolate shavings.

ROASTED VEGGIE PLATTER

There is nothing better than having veggies on hand and ready-to-go for snacking or serving them up in meals.

Roasting veggies will also give you a reason to not let anything sit in the back of the fridge and go to waste.

Serves 4

2 zucchini, sliced

1 1/2 cups cubed carrots

2 yellow squash, sliced

1 sweet potato, peeled and cubed

2 bell peppers of choice (red, green, yellow, or orange), sliced into sticks

1 yellow onion, sliced

1 red onion, sliced

1/4 cup extra virgin olive oil

3 tablespoons onion powder

3 tablespoons garlic powder

3 tablespoons fresh or dried parsley

2 teaspoons paprika

Salt and pepper, to taste

Preheat oven to 375 degrees. Line a baking sheet with parchment paper and spray with nonstick cooking spray.

Arrange vegetables in a single layer on baking sheet.

Drizzle with oil and sprinkle with onion powder, garlic powder, parsley, and paprika. Season with salt and pepper. Be sure to evenly distribute the oil and seasoning to coat veggies.

Bake for 40 minutes, or until veggies are tender.

KID HELP

- When the veggies are cut and prepped, let your child arrange them on the baking sheet.
- When all the seasonings and spices are added, let the kids mix it all up with a spoon so the veggies are evenly coated. It doesn't have to be perfect.

STEAMED MAPLE-MUSTARD KALE

Doesn't goodness plus goodness equal awesomeness? Well this fits the bill with its anti-inflammatory, immune boosting, cholesterol lowering, and high antioxidant properties. These three ingredients together serve up one heck of a tasty snack all while feeding the soul. Besides, who can say no to the King of Greens. Can I get a Kale Yea?

Serves 4

1 pound chopped fresh or frozen kale

⅓ cup maple syrup

2 to 3 tablespoons prepared yellow mustard

Salt and pepper, to taste

Using your preferred method, steam kale until soft, 10–12 minutes.

Transfer to a bowl with the maple syrup, mustard, salt, and pepper. Stir until coated.

Serve this in a bowl as a snack, or you can make it part of a meal by stuffing it inside baked sweet potatoes.

 **KID HELP**

- Have your child mix up the kale, maple syrup, and mustard in a bowl.
- If you are serving the kale with sweet potatoes, let your child stuff their own potato with the kale mixture. And if they want to add a drizzle more of maple syrup, let them have at it.

CHOCOLATE-BANANA ROLL-UPS

Chocolate and bananas, I mean is there a better combo? Everyone knows bananas are high in potassium, but did you know bananas also can put you in a good mood? So enjoying some of these roll ups will have the entire family smiling. And don't go light on the chocolate!

12 to 14 roll-ups or serves 2 to 3

- 2 (8-inch or 10-inch) flour tortillas
- 3 tablespoons melted dairy-free chocolate bar or chocolate chips
- 2 bananas, peeled

Spread tortillas with melted chocolate. Place 1 banana in the center of each tortilla. Roll up tightly.

Cut banana rolls into 1-inch-thick slices. Alternatively, you can cut each roll-up in half diagonally.

KID HELP

- Let your child spread the melted chocolate on their tortilla and place the bananas in the middle. (Parents do the cutting.)
- Let the kids get a little messy and enjoy this yummy snack.

FUDGE POPS

These fudge pops are a healthy spin on my childhood summer fave. They are loaded with a powerhouse of nutrients like cacao powder that's great for heart health and coconut milk that helps build muscle. All this while not taking away from the traditional taste of the choco-latey fudge!

Makes 12 pops

2 (13-ounce) cans full-fat coconut milk

$2/3$ cup cacao or cocoa powder

5 tablespoons maple syrup

2 teaspoons vanilla extract

Pinch of salt

Place all ingredients into a high-speed blender. Blend for 1 minute until completely smooth. Taste and adjust sweetening if needed.

Pour the fudge into ice pop molds and freeze for at least 4 hours or overnight.

Just before serving, run bottom of molds under warm water to loosen.

Note: I like to make these a day ahead. For a creamier texture, let the mixture sit in the blender for a half hour before pouring into molds. Give the mixture one good blitz then proceed.

KID HELP

- Let the kids add all ingredients to the blender.
- Have them pour it into the ice pop molds.
- When the pops are ready, have your child help remove the pops from the mold.

HONEYDEW ICE POPS

Honeydew melons are ninety percent water, are an excellent source of vitamin C, and have just as much potassium as a banana. Add some mint leaves and you've got yourself a nourishing yet refreshing yummy ice pop!

Makes 6 pops

$^1/_2$ honeydew melon, chopped

1 tablespoon maple syrup

$^1/_4$ cup coconut water

1 handful chopped fresh mint leaves, optional

Hemp seeds, to garnish

Place honeydew, syrup, and coconut water into a high-speed blender. Blend until combined.

Mix in mint leaves then pour melon mixture into ice pop molds and freeze for at least 4 hours or overnight.

Just before serving, run bottom of molds under warm water to loosen. Sprinkle tops of melon pops with hemp seeds.

Note: I like to make these a day ahead. You can add 1 frozen banana to the mix if desired.

KID HELP

- When you're done cutting up the melon, let the kids throw the pieces into the blender.
- Have them pour the mixture into the ice pop molds.
- When the pops are ready, have your child help remove the pops from the mold.

SPLURGE ALERT

BANANA ICE CREAM WITH COOKIES AND CREAM SWIRL

Dreamy banana ice cream mixed with chocolate sandwich cookies, oh my! This creamy sensation's main ingredient is bananas. You can opt out of using the cookies so this can be a healthy snack option instead of a splurge alert. But I urge you to have the splurge, because well, why not? Balance is key!

Serves 2 to 4

2 bananas, frozen

1/4 cup coconut milk

6 Oreos or other vegan chocolate sandwich cookies, crushed, plus extra whole cookies for serving

Homemade Healthy Chocolate Sauce (page 198)

Line a standard loaf pan with plastic wrap or parchment paper.

In a food processor or high-speed blender, blend the frozen bananas. They will be crumbly at first; keep blending until creamy. Add the coconut milk and continue blending. You don't want it the consistency of a smoothie, it should be more like soft-serve yogurt or ice cream.

Transfer mixture into a large bowl and mix in the crushed cookies. Pour into the loaf pan and freeze for at least 2 hours to set.

When the ice cream is set, scoop out and serve with extra cookies and a chocolate drizzle!

KID HELP

- You can have your child crumble up the cookies with their hands (I know, a bit messy) and pour them into the ice cream.
- When the ice cream is ready, let them top it with some chocolate sauce.

SALTED CHOCOLATE-ALMOND-COCONUT BARK

Guilt-free chocolate anyone? This is ridiculously fast and easy to make. You can opt to make it a superfood bark by using cacao powder instead of cocoa powder. This melt-in-your-mouth chocolate is sweetened with maple syrup and has a hint of salt, making this the perfect sweet treat.

Makes 20 to 24 pieces

1 cup cocoa powder

1 cup maple syrup

1 cup coconut oil, melted

1 cup shredded coconut

1 cup sliced almonds

Pink Himalayan rock salt

Spray a baking sheet with nonstick cooking spray. Line with parchment paper. (The spray will help the paper to stick.)

In a large bowl, whisk together the cocoa powder and maple syrup. Add in the coconut oil, a little bit at a time, whisking constantly. Fold in the coconut and almonds.

Pour mixture onto baking sheet and smooth out evenly with a spatula. Sprinkle with salt.

Place in the freezer for at least 1 hour, and preferably 4 hours, to set. Remove from freezer and break into pieces.

Note: This keeps well in the freezer or refrigerator for up to 2 weeks in an airtight container. If keeping in the freezer, let thaw for a few minutes before serving.

KID HELP

- While you're whisking together the cocoa powder, maple syrup, and coconut oil, let your child add in the coconut shreds and almonds.
- When the bark has set, allow them to break it into pieces.

POPCORN CAULIFLOWER

Cauliflower is one of the most versatile vegetables out there. It's also a great rice substitute, it's gluten free, and low carb. This popcorn spin on cauliflower takes this mega player to a whole new level.

Serves 2 to 4

1 cup coconut milk or organic soy milk

1 teaspoon apple cider vinegar

3/4 cup all-purpose flour

2 tablespoons nutritional yeast

2 teaspoons chili powder

Salt and pepper, to taste

1 head cauliflower, cut into florets

2 cups Italian breadcrumbs

1/2 cup or more extra virgin olive oil or organic canola oil for frying

In a large bowl, whisk together the coconut milk and vinegar; let set for 5 minutes. Meanwhile, line a plate with paper towels and set aside.

After 5 minutes, add the flour, nutritional yeast, and chili powder to the milk mixture; season with salt and pepper. Whisk until smooth.

Submerge each cauliflower floret into the batter then toss around in the breadcrumbs.

Heat oil in a large frying pan over medium heat. Fry cauliflower for 3–4 minutes, until golden brown and crispy all around. Transfer to the paper towel-lined plate and season with salt, pepper, and parsley.

Serve with ketchup or your favorite vegan ranch dressing.

Note: For a healthier version, bake the cauliflower. Preheat oven to 375 degrees. Line a baking sheet with parchment paper. Place the coated cauliflower on the baking sheet and bake for 25–30 minutes, until golden brown and crispy.

KID HELP

- Have your kids help by letting them dip the cauliflower into the batter and breadcrumbs.
- This can be messy, so have your little helpers assist with the cleanup.

HEALTHIER ONION RINGS

Onions are one of the healthiest veggies out there. They're known to detox the liver and kidneys, and they can even be used to fight against colds and the flu. But their amazingness doesn't stop there, they're also one tasty snack—making these healthier onion rings a sure winner!

Serves 2 to 4

2 large yellow onions, cut into $1/2$-inch slices

$1/2$ cup all-purpose flour

$1/2$ cup cornmeal

2 teaspoons baking powder

3 flax eggs (page 23)

$1/4$ cup organic soy milk or coconut milk

1 cup Italian breadcrumbs

1 tablespoon Cajun seasoning

Salt and pepper, to taste

Extra virgin olive oil spray

Preheat oven to 450 degrees. Line 2 baking sheets with parchment paper and spray with nonstick cooking spray.

Place onions into a bowl and cover completely with cold water. Set aside.

Combine the flour, cornmeal, and baking powder in a bowl. In another bowl, combine the flax eggs and milk; mix well. In a third bowl, combine the breadcrumbs, seasoning, and salt and pepper.

Take 1 onion slice out of the water, shaking off the excess. Dredge in flour mixture; shake off excess, and dip in the egg mixture. Coat in the breadcrumb mixture. Place on baking sheet and repeat with remaining onions.

When ready to bake, spray all rings with olive oil spray. Bake for 10 minutes, flip onions and bake for another 10 minutes until evenly baked on both sides.

Serve with a side of ketchup!

 **KID HELP**

- Have your kids help coat the onion rings.
- Have them place the prepared onion rings on the baking sheet.

APPLE PIE ROLL-UPS

Are you an apple person? I'm an apple person, and these little apple pie sandwiches are perfectly sized, tender, and have just the right amount of sweetness. It's like eating a homemade apple pie with every single bite.

Serves 4 to 8

- 1 package (8 rolls) refrigerated vegan crescent rolls
- 1 Granny Smith apple, cored and diced
- 1 Gala apple, cored and diced
- 1/4 cup coconut sugar
- 1 teaspoon cinnamon
- 1/4 teaspoon nutmeg
- 1/2 teaspoon apple cider vinegar
- 1/4 cup water
- 1/2 teaspoon vegan butter, melted, optional

Preheat oven according to crescent roll package instructions. Line a baking sheet with parchment paper.

In a saucepan over medium heat, add the apples, sugar, cinnamon, nutmeg, vinegar, and water. Cook for about 8 minutes, stirring occasionally, until thickened. Purée half of the apple mixture in a food processor. Add back to remaining apple mixture.

Arrange the crescent roll triangles on the prepared baking sheet. Place 1/2 tablespoon of apple mixture on the wide end of a triangle. Roll the triangle around the mixture, starting at the shortest point and rolling toward the opposite side. Repeat until all rolls are filled.

Lightly brush tops of rolls with butter and bake according to package instructions. Let cool for 5 minutes before serving.

Note: You can ice the tops of the rolls for mini apple turnovers. You'll need 1 cup powdered sugar and 2 tablespoons almond milk. Mix to desired consistency and drizzle lightly over top.

KID HELP

- When you're finished making the apple mixture, have your kids unravel the crescent rolls and spoon in the apple mixture then roll them up.
- When the rolls are done baking, have them make the icing, and drizzle it over apple sandwiches.

DINNERS

"DINNER SHOULDN'T BE SKIPPED"

Just as breakfast and lunch are a necessity to start the day and get you through it, dinner has its importance just the same. Dinner shouldn't ever be skipped. What you eat is important for your body and your organs while you sleep. As adults we need at least seven hours of solid sleep. Our kids need anywhere between ten and twelve hours. Eating a meal full of plant-based protein, healthy carbs, and vitamin-rich veggies will aid in a peaceful night's sleep without interruption. No one wants to wake up Mr. Grumpy Pants!

ONE-SKILLET CHEESY PASTA

Using a homemade vegan cheese sauce and seasoned tempeh gives this meal the healthy twist it deserves. Ultra cheesy, kid and adult approved!

Serves 4 to 6

2 cups uncooked organic elbow macaroni

8 ounces organic tempeh

1 tablespoon extra virgin olive oil

1 cup marinara sauce

1 teaspoon paprika

1 teaspoon ground cumin

2 teaspoons fresh or dried parsley

Salt and pepper, to taste

1 1/2 cups The Best Vegan Cheese Wiz (page 193)

1/2 yellow onion, diced

1 cup green onions, diced

1 red bell pepper, diced

Prepare the pasta according to package instructions.

While the pasta cooks, chop up the tempeh into small pieces. Place into a large skillet with the oil. Cook over medium heat, using a spatula to break the tempeh into small pieces. When the tempeh has been broken up, add the marinara, paprika, cumin, and parsley; season with salt and pepper.

Add 2 cups pasta to the tempeh mixture along with the cheese sauce, yellow and green onions, and bell pepper.

Stir everything well and adjust seasonings to your liking. Keep stirring over low to medium heat for 5 minutes.

Serve immediately and enjoy! This keeps well in the refrigerator in an airtight container for up to 4 days.

KID HELP

- Let your child help you prepare the cheese sauce.
- When the pasta is done, let them mix the pasta, cheese, and tempeh all together.

ONE-POT MUSHROOM PASTA

This delicious, creamy mushroom pasta is not only cooked and ready to eat all in one pot in under 20 minutes; it's also super high in antioxidants thanks to all the mushrooms!

Serves 6

4 1/2 cups water

1 pound quinoa and brown rice spaghetti

1 pound cremini mushrooms, sliced

2 zucchini, halved lengthwise and quartered into 16 pieces

1 pound frozen or fresh peas

2 cloves garlic, sliced

3 teaspoons dried thyme

1 tablespoon nutritional yeast

Salt and pepper, to taste

1 tablespoon coconut butter or other vegan butter

1/4 cup almond milk

1 tablespoon brown rice flour, optional

Deliciously Easy Vegan Parmesan Cheese (page 189), to taste

In a large pot, combine the water, spaghetti, mushrooms, zucchini, peas, garlic, thyme, and nutritional yeast; season with salt and pepper.

Bring to a boil then reduce to a simmer. As soon as the pasta is at the simmer stage, stir in the milk and butter. Let simmer for 8–10 minutes, making sure to keep an eye on the pasta so that it doesn't stick together.

The liquid should be somewhat reduced at this point. If it's still a little too watery and you want it thicker, stir in the flour.

Remove from heat and let stand for 5 minutes, giving it a good stir before serving. Serve sprinkled with Parmesan.

KID HELP

- Have your child help you prep the veggies, whether it's cleaning or cutting them.
- Let them give the pasta a good stir before serving it and topping it with the cheese.

VEGAN ALFREDO BOW TIES

Don't be surprised when everyone is reaching for seconds. This vegan Alfredo sauce comes to win! It is super creamy and thick just like traditional Alfredo except we nixed the cream, butter, and cheese. The subbed healthier, better for you ingredients don't take anything away from the classic rich taste.

Serves 4 to 6

1 pound farfalle pasta

$2\frac{1}{2}$ cups unsweetened almond milk

$2\frac{1}{2}$ tablespoons brown rice flour

$1\frac{1}{2}$ tablespoons nutritional yeast

$1\frac{1}{2}$ teaspoons Bragg Liquid Aminos

1 tablespoon garlic powder

1 tablespoon onion powder

2 tablespoons coconut butter

1 teaspoon yellow mustard

1 teaspoon Himalayan pink salt

1 cup frozen or fresh peas, steamed or parboiled

Prepare the pasta according to package directions.

While you are preparing the pasta, make the Alfredo. In a saucepan over low to medium heat, whisk together the almond milk, flour, nutritional yeast, aminos, garlic powder, onion powder, coconut butter, mustard, and salt. Cook, stirring occasionally, for 5 minutes.

Bring to a simmer and stir frequently for about 8 minutes, until mixture starts to thicken. Remove from heat.

Drain pasta then toss with sauce and peas.

 **KID HELP**

- Let the kids prepare the pasta with your guidance.
- Have them help make the Alfredo sauce.
- Let them pour the sauce over the pasta and toss in the peas.

PIZZA (NOT POTATO) SKINS

Since cauliflower is extremely low carb, sugar free, and essentially has no fat but packs a nutritional punch in the wellness department, you know it's a veggie you need to be hanging out with more often. This recipe brings regular potato skins to the next healthy level.

Serves 6 to 8

1 head cauliflower

2 tablespoons vegan butter

$1/2$ cup almond milk

Salt and pepper, to taste

Onion powder, to taste

Garlic powder, to taste

1 clove garlic

1 (8-inch) frozen Vicolo Corn Meal Pizza Crust

Vegan mozzarella cheese shreds, for topping

Vegan bacon bits, for topping

Handful chopped scallions or green onions, for topping

Vegan Sour Cream (page 184), for topping

Boil or steam the cauliflower. In a blender, add the cauliflower, butter, milk, seasonings, and garlic; blend to desired mashed consistency.

Preheat oven and prepare the pizza crust according to package directions.

Spread the cauliflower mash evenly across the crust. Sprinkle mozzarella over top and return to the oven for about 5 minutes, until cheese is melted.

Sprinkle with the bacon bits, scallions, and a dollop of sour cream.

Note: You can use any pizza crust you prefer! Just make sure it is about 8 inches.

KID HELP

- Have your child assist in making the cauliflower mash.
- When your crust and cauli mash are ready to go, let your child spread the mash across the cornmeal crust and top with all desired fixings.

MY GO-TO EASY SPAGHETTI SQUASH RECIPE

Want something other than pasta? Well this recipe uses garlic, olive oil, and vegan butter to make it one of the easiest, most delicious ways to enjoy this vegetable.

Serves 2

1 medium spaghetti squash

1 tablespoon extra virgin olive oil

1 1/2 tablespoons onion powder, or to taste

1 1/2 tablespoons garlic powder, or to taste

1 1/2 tablespoons dried parsley, plus extra

Salt and pepper, to taste

2 tablespoons vegan butter

Preheat oven to 350 degrees. Line a baking sheet with parchment paper.

Cut squash lengthwise and remove the seeds. (See note for an alternative way to open.) Using a fork, poke holes into the skin. Pour the oil over both sides of squash and rub it in with your hands.

Season the cut sides with onion powder, garlic powder, parsley, and salt and pepper; place, skin side down, on the baking sheet.

Bake for 45–50 minutes, until easily pierced with a fork. Remove from oven. When cool enough to touch, shred squash with a fork and place into a bowl. Dot squash with butter and sprinkle with more parsley if desired. Serve and enjoy!

Note: If you have a hard time cutting spaghetti squash open while raw, you can cook it first. Poke a few holes in the skin and bake at 350 degrees for 45–50 minutes. Let cool. Then cut it in half, remove the seeds, and season as desired.

KID HELP

- Let your child season the squash before it goes into the oven.
- When the squash is ready and is cool to touch, let your child shred the inside with a fork.

MUSHROOM FLATBREAD PIZZA

Made with organic ingredients, home-made dough, faux cheese, and a whole-lotta toppings, this is the ultimate pizza for plant lovers.

Serves 6 to 8

Flatbread

2 teaspoons active dry yeast

2 teaspoons Italian seasoning

Pinch of salt

$1^1/_2$ cups warm water

$3^1/_4$ cups bread flour or white whole-wheat flour

Toppings

$1^1/_2$ cups white button mushrooms, sliced

2 tablespoons vegan butter, divided

3 cloves garlic, thinly sliced

1 cup almond milk

1 tablespoon brown rice flour or all-purpose flour

Salt and pepper, to taste

$1/_2$ cup vegan mozzarella cheese shreds, plus extra, optional

1 cup steamed broccoli

1 cup mixed greens (such as kale, spinach, and mustard greens)

Flatbread

In a large bowl, combine all the ingredients. Mix well and knead by hand, or use a stand mixer with a dough hook, until smooth and pliable. Place dough in lightly greased bowl, cover, and let rise at room temperature for 1 hour.

Line a baking sheet with parchment paper. Set aside. Lightly flour work surface and roll out dough into a rectangle. Transfer dough to the baking sheet, pressing to the edges.

Toppings

In a skillet, sauté the mushrooms and garlic in 1 tablespoon butter for 5–8 minutes, until mushrooms are browned.

In a saucepan over medium heat, add milk, flour, salt and pepper, and remaining butter. Stir constantly for about 3 minutes until thickened. Remove from heat and add $1/_2$ cup cheese. Mix well to melt the cheese.

Preheat oven to 400 degrees.

Spread the sauce over the dough, leaving a $1^1/_2$-inch border. Top with broccoli, greens, and mushrooms; sprinkle with more cheese if desired. Bake for 20–25 minutes, until the cheese is melty and the crust is golden.

 KID HELP

- When the dough is rolled out, let them pour the cheese sauce on the dough then place the veggies on top.

HOMEMADE VEGGIE NUGGETS

Buh-bye fast food nuggets and hello tasty little veg gems. Loaded with nutritious veggies, these come ready to party, allowing kids and parents to enjoy the best of both worlds—double win!

Serves 10 to 12

1 $1/2$ cups Italian breadcrumbs, divided

$1/2$ cup broccoli florets

$1/2$ cup chickpeas (garbanzo beans), drained, rinsed, and patted dry

1 cup shredded carrots

2 cloves garlic

2 tablespoons nutritional yeast

1 tablespoon dried parsley

1 teaspoon onion powder

1 teaspoon garlic powder

1 flax egg (page 23)

Salt and pepper, to taste

2 to 3 tablespoons avocado oil or other heat-friendly oil, for frying

Ketchup or vegan honey mustard, for dipping

Place $1/2$ cup breadcrumbs into a bowl and set aside.

Bring a small pot of water to a boil. Cook the broccoli until tender, about 8 minutes. Drain and transfer to a food processor.

Add the chickpeas, carrots, remaining breadcrumbs, garlic, nutritional yeast, parsley, onion powder, garlic powder, and flax egg to the food processor; season with salt and pepper. Pulse until a fine mixture forms. If too crumbly, add a bit of water or oil, 1 teaspoon at a time, until the mixture holds together.

Heat the oil over medium heat in a skillet.

Take tablespoon-size portions of veggie mixture and roll into balls then gently flatten into nugget shapes. Roll nuggets in reserved breadcrumbs.

Fry for 5 minutes on each side, or until crispy and golden brown. Transfer to paper towels to drain. Serve with ketchup or a vegan honey mustard.

Note: Alternatively, you can bake the nuggets. Preheat oven to 350 degrees and place them on a baking sheet lined with parchment paper. Bake for 25–30 minutes or until golden.

KID HELP

- Let your child assist you in preparing the veggie mix.
- Have them form the nuggets into desired shapes and hand them to you to fry, or place them on the baking sheet.

BAKED MAC 'N' CHEESE

 SPLURGE ALERT

This baked mac 'n' cheese is loaded with an insanely good, smooth vegan cheese sauce mixed with elbow pasta.

The breadcrumbs add a much needed crunch, making this the ultimate vegan comfort food.

Serves 4

1 pound elbow pasta

2 cups or more The Best Vegan Cheese Wiz (page 193)

1 cup Italian breadcrumbs

1 teaspoon paprika

1 handful Deliciously Easy Vegan Parmesan Cheese (page 189), optional

Applesauce, for serving, optional

Cook pasta according to package instructions. Drain and transfer to a large bowl. Pour about half of the cheese sauce into the pasta, reserving the other half; stir well.

Preheat oven to 350 degrees.

Pour the mac 'n' cheese filling into an 8 x 10-inch baking dish. Sprinkle the breadcrumbs and paprika over top.

Pour about $1/3$ cup of the reserved cheese around the sides of the dish only. There will be cheese leftover.

Bake for 15 minutes. If desired, you can turn on the broiler for 5 minutes to crisp the top.

When serving, pour the leftover cheese sauce over the top of the baked macaroni. Sprinkle with Parmesan and serve with a side of applesauce.

 KID HELP

- Let your kids help you make the cheese sauce.
- When the pasta is done, let your child pour the cheese sauce over the pasta and mix well.
- Let them sprinkle the Parmesan on the top.

MASHED CAULIFLOWER

Mashed potatoes are typically a staple for dinner gatherings. My family makes tons of mash with gravy. Instead, I make cauliflower mash. The texture is pretty much the same, yet it has a third of the calories than potatoes, and a fourth of the carbs!

Serves 2 to 4

1 large head cauliflower

2 to 3 cloves garlic, minced

3 tablespoons vegan butter

1/4 cup almond milk, plus extra

Salt and pepper, to taste

1 tablespoon dried parsley

Clean and rinse the cauliflower and cut into florets. Steam or boil cauliflower for 10 minutes, or until tender. Drain well.

Place cauliflower in a food processor and pulse until it forms a rice-like texture.

Add the remaining ingredients and pulse to desired mash consistency. Add more milk if you like a smooth, creamy mash.

Note: If you don't have a food processor, no worries. You can mash cauliflower with a fork and fold in all ingredients. A hand mixer would work just as well too.

KID HELP

- Have your child help you clean the cauliflower and separate the florets from the core.
- Have them assist you by placing cauliflower in the food processor and watching it turn into rice!
- Have your child help with adding the rest of the ingredients to make the mash.

ROASTED SWEET POTATO BITES

These sweet immune boosting bites can be served as a snack or side. Coming in high with antioxidants, they are great paired with Steamed Maple-Mustard Kale (page 108),

Serves 2 to 4

2 to 3 large sweet potatoes, peeled and cut into 1- to 2-inch cubes

Coconut oil nonstick spray, or 1 tablespoon coconut oil, melted

2 tablespoons maple syrup

2 teaspoons cinnamon

Preheat oven to 350 degrees. Line a baking sheet with parchment paper

Spread potatoes evenly across the baking sheet. Spray with the cooking spray or drizzle with oil. Pour syrup over top and sprinkle with cinnamon. Stir to coat evenly, adding more maple syrup or cinnamon, if desired.

Bake for 30 minutes, stirring after 15 minutes. Remove from oven and enjoy!

KID HELP

- After you're done cutting the potatoes into cubes, let your child sprinkle them with cinnamon, coconut oil, and maple syrup.
- Have them toss the bites around so they're evenly coated.

BAKED BROCCOLI TATER TOTS

Broccoli is a powerful green veggie that's super heart healthy, has as ton of vitamin C, and keeps skin glowing and fresh looking. So not only are these a breeze to make, and the kids love them, their benefits are endless for all ages.

Serves 4

1 large russet potato, peeled and chopped

2 cups broccoli florets

1/4 cup nutritional yeast

1/2 small yellow onion, diced

1/3 cup vegan cheddar cheese shreds

1/2 cup Italian breadcrumbs

2 tablespoons dried parsley

Salt and pepper, to taste

Ketchup, for dipping

Preheat oven to 375 degrees. Line a baking sheet with parchment paper.

Bring a pot of water to a boil. Add the potato and broccoli and boil for 6 minutes.

Remove veggies from water, drain, and place in a food processor. Pulse a few times to finely grate, and transfer to a large bowl. Pop in the remaining ingredients (except ketchup) and mix well.

Using your hands, take a heaping tablespoon of the mixture, squeeze it gently, roll it into a ball, and then form into a tater tot shape. Place on the baking sheet. Repeat this step until all the mixture is gone.

Bake for 20–25 minutes, until golden edges appear. Let cool for 5–10 minutes before serving. Add a side of ketchup to dip!

 **KID HELP**

- Have your child mix all ingredients after the potato and broccoli have been grated.
- Let them shape the broccoli mixture into tot-like shapes. It doesn't have to be perfect, this is the fun part.

PIZZA ROLLS

It literally doesn't get any easier than pizza rolls. All this super vegan cheesy goodness and sauciness rolled up together lands these rolls in the dinner rotation weekly as a must make. And no one is judging if you make this twice in one week—I totally get it!

Serves 8

1 (8-roll) package refrigerated vegan crescent rolls or ready-made pizza dough

$1/2$ cup pizza or marinara sauce, plus extra

$1^1/2$ cups vegan mozzarella shreds

Toppings of choice: mushrooms, olives, spinach, pineapple, etc.

Preheat oven to 350 degrees. Line a baking sheet with parchment paper.

Roll the crescent roll dough out on a flat surface, pressing the seams together to form 1 large rectangle. If using pizza dough, roll out into a large rectangle.

Spread the pizza sauce over the dough, leaving a $1/2$-inch border. Top with mozzarella and any other toppings of choice.

Roll dough up lengthwise then slice into 1-inch-thick pieces. Place on the baking sheet and bake for 12–15 minutes, until tops are golden brown. Let cool for 5 minutes then serve with extra pizza sauce for dipping!

KID HELP

- Let your child prepare the rolls with desired fillings, pizza sauce, vegan cheese, mushrooms, etc.
- Have them roll up the dough and place cut pieces on baking sheet.

ITALIAN HOLIDAY SOUP

This is my absolute favorite soup recipe, which has become a holiday family staple. And if someone comes down with a cold, this is my go-to broth to make them feel better because of its many anti-inflammatory properties.

Serves 8 to 10

4 tablespoons vegan butter

$1/2$ cup extra virgin olive oil

5 cloves garlic, minced

1 large yellow onion

$2^1/2$ cups sliced carrots

3 cups diced celery

4 cups water, plus extra if needed

8 cups (64 ounces) low-sodium vegetable broth, plus extra if needed

6 ounces tomato paste

2 cubes vegetable bouillon

2 cubes vegan "chicken" bouillon

$1/2$ cup nutritional yeast

$1/4$ cup dried parsley

$1/4$ cup dried basil

$1/4$ cup dried oregano

$1/4$ cup onion powder

$1/4$ cup garlic powder

Salt and pepper, to taste

1 cup acini di pepe or pastina pasta

In a large soup pot over medium heat, melt the butter and oil. Add the garlic and onions and cook until onions are translucent. Add the carrots and celery. Mix well. Cover and cook for 10 minutes, stirring occasionally.

Add the broth and water and bring to a boil. Add the tomato paste, bouillon, and seasonings. Lower heat to medium, stirring frequently.

When the tomato paste and bouillon have been absorbed into the broth, stir in the pasta. Continue cooking for 20 minutes, stirring frequently so the pasta doesn't stick to the bottom of the pot. Reduce heat to low and simmer for 30 minutes, stirring occasionally. Taste and adjust seasonings.

The broth will thicken up because of the pasta. If you prefer more broth, you can add about 1 cup vegetable broth or water. When heating up leftovers you may find it necessary to add more liquid.

 **KID HELP**

- Let your child assist with cleaning the vegetables.
- With guidance, let them cut some of the veggies. If they are too young to use a knife, you can give them a play knife, a small cutting board, and a few pieces of vegetables. This involves them in the process.

CORN, BEAN, AND CHEESE TAQUITOS

This is a kid FAVE and that makes us parents super happy. Why? Because they're so easy to make yet completely filled with a ton of nutritious veggies!

Swapping out the frying part for baking, these are great as an after school snack, too.

Serves 4 to 6

1 1/2 cups fresh or frozen and thawed sweet corn

1 (15-ounce) can vegan refried beans

1 small yellow onion, diced

1/2 cup vegan cheddar cheese shreds, plus extra to top

10 to 12 (8- or 10-inch) flour tortillas

1 avocado, sliced

1/2 cup fresh cilantro

Lime wedges

1/2 cup Vegan Sour Cream (page 184) or store bought

In a small or medium saucepan, boil corn until tender, 10–12 minutes. Remove from heat; drain. In a large skillet, combine the beans, onion, cheese, and corn. Cook until cheese has melted; remove from heat.

Preheat oven to 375 degrees. Line a baking sheet with parchment paper.

Spread 2 tablespoons of bean mixture down the middle of 1 tortilla. Roll up tightly and place seam side down on the baking sheet. Repeat with remaining tortillas and filling. Lightly spray taquitos with olive oil spray. If desired, top with cheese. Bake for 10 minutes, or until slightly golden brown.

Top with avocado slices, a sprinkle of cilantro, and a squeeze of lime. Serve with sour cream.

KID HELP

- Let your child combine the veggies and cheese.
- Have them fill and roll the tortillas and place on baking sheet.

DECONSTRUCTED SLOPPY JOE OVER RICE

This classic kid-friendly recipe is a family favorite. You can serve it up on a bun or swap out the rice for a pasta made with quinoa, lentil, or whole grain. You can switch it up, allowing you to enjoy this meal in many ways!

Serves 6 to 8

1 cup short- or long-grain uncooked white rice

1 tablespoon extra virgin olive oil or avocado oil

1 yellow onion, diced

2 cloves garlic, minced

¼ cup chopped celery

2 (8-ounce) packages tempeh, finely chopped

1 cup ketchup

1 tablespoon vegan Worcestershire sauce

1 teaspoon yellow mustard

½ tablespoon maple syrup

Salt and pepper, to taste

Cook rice according to package directions while preparing the Sloppy Joe mixture.

Heat oil in a skillet over medium heat, and add onion, garlic, and celery. Cook until tender, about 6 minutes. Add tempeh and stir. Cook until heated through, 10–15 minutes. Then add in the ketchup, Worcestershire sauce, mustard, syrup, and salt and pepper. Mix well to thoroughly combine; cook another 8–10 minutes.

To serve, scoop ½ cup rice on individual serving plates then top with the Sloppy Joe mixture. Serve with a side salad or other green vegetable like broccoli or spinach.

Notes: You can use instant rice if you want to save time.

To make Sloppy Joes in the traditional style, you'll need 4 to 6 hamburger buns. Fill them up and have at it.

KID HELP

- Have your child assist you in making the Sloppy Joe mixture.
- Let them assemble their own plates with whatever they prefer, rice, pasta, or a bun. Intended to be messy!

SWEET POTATO CASSEROLE

This is another classic staple come the holidays. With its sweet crunchy middle and gooey melty top, this is a smooth dish best served with love.

Serves 6 to 8

4 to 5 large sweet potatoes, peeled and chopped

1/2 cup maple syrup

3 tablespoons vegan butter

1/3 cup almond milk

2 teaspoons cinnamon

2 teaspoons vanilla extract

1 cup chopped pecans, optional

Pinch of salt

Vegan marshmallows, to top

Bring a large pot of water to a boil. Add the potatoes and cook until tender, about 25 minutes.

Preheat oven to 350 degrees. Prepare and 8 x 8-inch baking dish with coconut oil spray.

Drain potatoes and transfer to a large bowl. Mash to desired consistency then add the syrup, butter, milk, cinnamon, vanilla, pecans, and salt; mix until well-combined. Taste and adjust sweetness if needed. If you'd like to thin the mixture, add 1 tablespoon of maple syrup or almond milk.

Place sweet potato mixture into baking dish and generously cover the top with marshmallows.

Bake for 15–20 minutes. If you want the top a little charred, place the baking dish under the broiler for 3–5 minutes. This will roast and melt down the marshmallows; vegan marshmallows don't melt as quickly as traditional marshmallows.

Remove from oven, let cool for a couple of minutes, and then serve with an extra drizzle of maple syrup.

KID HELP

- Have your child mash the potatoes once they are cool and add in syrup, butter, milk, cinnamon, vanilla, and pecans.
- Let them top the casserole with marshmallows.

STUFFED PEPPERS

Bell peppers are amazing in so many ways. Not only can they counterbalance the destructive effects of free radicals in our body, they are deeelicious!

Serves 4 to 8

4 green bell peppers

Salt, to taste

4 cups water

2 cups uncooked white rice

2 tablespoons extra virgin olive oil

2 cloves garlic, minced

1 yellow onion, diced

1 cup fresh or frozen corn kernels

1 cup sliced black olives

2 cups marinara sauce, divided, plus extra

2 teaspoons onion powder

2 teaspoons garlic powder

2 teaspoons dried basil

2 teaspoons dried oregano

2 teaspoons dried parsley

Salt and pepper, to taste

1 cup vegan mozzarella shreds, plus extra

Deliciously Easy Vegan Parmesan Cheese (page 189), to taste

Preheat oven to 350 degrees. Cut the tops off the peppers. Remove ribs and seeds. Trim and chop pepper around the stems. Sprinkle some salt inside each pepper and set aside.

In a pot, bring water to a boil. Add rice, reduce heat, and simmer, covered, for 20–25 minutes. Remove from heat and fluff with a fork.

Heat the oil in a large skillet over medium heat. Add the garlic, onion, and chopped peppers; cook until onion is translucent, about 5 minutes. Stir in the corn, olives, 1 cup marinara, onion and garlic powder, basil, oregano, and parsley; season with salt and pepper. Once warmed, stir in 1 cup of rice and cheese. Taste and adjust seasonings.

In an 8 x 8-inch baking dish, pour in remaining marinara sauce. Generously stuff each pepper with filling. Stand peppers in baking dish. The sauce should reach halfway up the pepper, so add more if needed. Pour extra marinara over the tops and sprinkle with cheeses. Bake for 25–30 minutes, until peppers are tender.

Note: For super soft peppers, steam them for 10–15 minutes before stuffing. For extra plant-based protein, you can substitute quinoa for rice!

KID HELP

- Let your child help stuff the peppers.
- Have the kids place the peppers carefully in the baking dish and pour in the remaining sauce.

BUTTERNUT SQUASH, SPINACH, AND BLACK BEAN ENCHILADAS

These loaded enchiladas come complete with a bright green salsa verde and a mildly spicy veggie mix creating an epic Mexican-American classic that doesn't leave you feeling overly full. They are at maximum capacity in the land of deliciousness.

Serves 8

- 2 cups cubed butternut squash
- 2 tablespoons extra virgin olive oil
- Salt and pepper, to taste
- 2 cups frozen spinach
- 1 (15-ounce) can black beans, drained and rinsed
- 1 teaspoon salt
- 1 teaspoon pepper
- 1 teaspoon onion powder

Preheat oven to 350 degrees. Line a baking sheet with parchment paper.

Spread squash on the baking sheet, toss with oil, sprinkle with salt and pepper, and bake for 20 minutes or until tender.

Meanwhile, steam the spinach for 10–12 minutes.

Transfer squash, spinach, and beans to a large bowl. Lightly season with 1 teaspoon salt, 1 teaspoon pepper, onion and garlic powder, and paprika.

Spread $1/4$ cup salsa verde on the bottom of a 9 x 13-inch baking dish. Soften the tortillas for a few seconds in the microwave. Place about $1/4$ to $1/3$ cup filling down the center of each tortilla. Add 1 tablespoon salsa verde, and a handful of cheese. Roll up and place seam side down in the baking

1 teaspoon garlic
  powder

1 teaspoon paprika

1$^{1}/_{2}$ cups salsa verde

6 to 8 (10-inch) corn
  tortillas

$^{1}/_{2}$ cup chopped fresh
  cilantro

Vegan cheese shreds, of
  choice

Vegan Sour Cream (page
  184)

Chopped fresh cilantro

Lime wedges

Sliced avocado

dish. Top with remaining salsa verde and another handful of cheese. Bake for 20–25 minutes until heated through and cheese is melted. Serve with sour cream, fresh cilantro, sprinkles of lime juice, and avocado slices.

KID HELP

- Let your child help toss vegetables and seasonings together.
- Have them fill the tortillas and place in baking dish.
- Let your kids add toppings as desired.

BUTTERY BAKED POTATO SMASHERS

This is the amped-up version of potato skins. Coated with garlic and melty butter, these are a go-to for a weeknight meal. Butter. In. Every. Bite. YUM!

Makes 12 smashers

12 red jacket potatoes

1/3 cup vegan butter, melted

2 cloves garlic, minced

Salt and pepper, to taste

Vegan Sour Cream (page 184) or store bought

1/2 cup chopped green onions

Preheat oven to 425 degrees. Line 2 baking sheets with parchment paper and spray with olive oil cooking spray.

Bring a large pot of salted water to a boil. Boil the potatoes until fork-tender, 8–10 minutes. Drain and let cool slightly.

Arrange potatoes on baking sheets. Gently smash them using the palm of your hand, a fork, or a potato masher until they are about 1 inch thick but still intact.

Combine the butter and garlic and brush potatoes; season with salt and pepper.

Bake for 25 minutes, turning the potatoes halfway through for even crispiness. Remove from oven and top with sour cream and onions.

KID HELP

- Let your child help smash the potatoes once they're cool to touch.
- Have them brush potatoes with butter mixture and pop in the oven.

BAKED ZITI

Baked Ziti is basically the lazy parent's lasagna, but still as equally delicious. You can get the same great taste and texture minus all the hard work, and enjoy this for dinner during the week without spending hours upon hours in the kitchen.

Serves 4 to 6

1 pound ziti

1 (25-ounce) jar marinara sauce (about 3 cups plus 2 tablespoons)

1 tablespoon dried parsley

$1/2$ tablespoon dried basil

$1/2$ tablespoon dried oregano

Salt and pepper, to taste

2 cups vegan mozzarella cheese shreds

Preheat oven to 350 degrees.

Prepare the pasta according to package instructions, drain and transfer to a 9 x 13-inch baking dish. Evenly pour the marinara sauce over the pasta.

Add the parsley, basil, and oregano; season with salt and pepper. Mix well, taste, and adjust seasonings as needed. Sprinkle the cheese over top. Bake for 20–25 minutes until cheese is melted and sauce is bubbling.

Serve with a side salad or green vegetables like steamed broccoli.

Note: You can add Cashew Ricotta Cheese (page 188) and Deliciously Easy Vegan Parmesan Cheese (page 189) on top for extra plant-based cheesiness.

KID HELP

- Have your child pour the pasta and marinara sauce in the baking dish.
- Have them add in the seasonings and cheese then give it a good mix.

SPAGHETTI AND LENTIL SAUCE

Lentils are a leading source of plant-based protein. Just one cup of cooked lentils contains eighteen grams of protein. This helps build muscle, gives you energy, and fuels you up properly, making it easy on the stomach to digest.

Serves 4 to 6

- 4 tablespoons extra virgin olive oil
- 1 yellow onion, chopped
- 4 cloves garlic, minced
- 2 cups chopped celery
- 1 cup sliced carrots
- 1 cup lentils
- 1 cup water
- 4 cups (32 ounces) low-sodium vegetable broth, plus extra
- 1 cube vegetable bouillon
- 1 tablespoon onion powder
- 1 tablespoon garlic powder
- Salt and pepper, to taste
- 1 pound spaghetti
- Deliciously Easy Vegan Parmesan Cheese (page 189)

In a large soup pot, heat the oil over medium-high heat. Add the onion and garlic and cook until fragrant and onion is translucent, about 5 minutes. Add the celery and carrots, cover, and let cook for 10 minutes, stirring occasionally.

Rinse and drain the lentils, picking through for any shriveled lentils, debris, or rocks.

Add the water, broth, bouillon, onion powder, garlic powder, and lentils to the pot. Season with salt and pepper. Stir. Bring to a rolling boil, reduce to a simmer, and cook for 30–40 minutes, stirring occasionally, until lentils are very tender. If they're still hard or snappy, they need to be cooked longer.

When lentils are done, add an additional 1 to 2 cups vegetable broth, if desired. Taste and adjust seasonings. Turn off heat, cover, and keep warm.

Prepare spaghetti according to package instructions. Drain.

Serve spaghetti in bowls and top with lentils and broth. Sprinkle Parmesan on top and enjoy!

KID HELP

- Have your kids assist you in preparing the carrots and celery.
- Let them help you add seasonings and cook the pasta.

DESSERTS

"MAKE WHAT YOU LOVE"

Desserts are a must! It's great to make things that you enjoy that don't sacrifice your health while eating it. Love chocolate cake? No problem! You can make what you love, and what your kids love, with better ingredients that actually do the body good. What better way to conclude a meal, or satisfy a craving, than with something nutritiously sweet!

ALMOND BUTTER-BANANA BREAD BLONDIES

These blondies are nutritious, full of delicious healthy fats and fiber, and most importantly, stuffed with creamy almond butter, bananas, and chocolate!

Serves 9

2 bananas, mashed

3/4 cup almond butter, plus extra

2 teaspoons vanilla extract

1/2 tablespoon coconut oil, melted

1/2 cup almond milk

1/3 cup coconut sugar

1 1/2 cups almond meal

3 tablespoons coconut flour

1 1/2 teaspoons baking powder

1 teaspoon baking soda

2 tablespoons cornstarch or arrowroot flour

Pinch of salt

1 cup carob chips or any other dairy-free chocolate chips

Preheat oven to 350 degrees. Prepare a 9 x 9-inch baking pan with nonstick cooking spray and line with parchment paper.

In a large bowl, mix together the bananas, almond butter, vanilla, oil, and milk until creamy. Add the sugar, almond meal, flour, baking powder, baking soda, cornstarch, and salt; mix well. Fold in carob chips.

Pour batter into pan and smooth top. Sprinkle more carob chips on top, if desired, and bake for 30–35 minutes, or until a toothpick inserted in the center comes out clean. Remove from oven and let cool in the pan for 5 minutes. Remove blondies from pan and cut into squares. If desired, heat 1 tablespoon of almond butter until melted and drizzle over blondies.

Store, covered, at room temperature or in the refrigerator.

Note: Some almond butters are oilier than others, so if necessary, reduce measure to 1/2 cup.

 **KID HELP**

- Let your kids mash up the bananas.
- Let them help mix batter.
- Before baking, let kids top sprinkle more carob chips over batter.

PEANUT BUTTER MOUSSE

This vitamin E-packed, nutrient-rich delicious creamy peanut buttery mousse is a dessert you can dig your spoon right into and feel good about eating.

Serves 4 to 6

2 (15-ounce) cans organic full-fat coconut milk, refrigerated for 24 hours

4 to 6 tablespoons maple syrup, or liquid sweetener of choice

2 teaspoons vanilla extract

6 tablespoons organic creamy or crunchy peanut butter

Dash of Himalayan pink rock salt (if peanut butter is unsalted)

Organic vegan peanut butter cups, optional

Organic vegan peanut butter chips, optional

Scoop out coconut cream from the cans and discard water, or save for later to use in smoothies.

In a large bowl, whip together the cream, syrup, vanilla, peanut butter, and salt until completely incorporated.

Portion mousse into dessert glasses, bowls, or however you want to enjoy this creamy deliciousness. Top with peanut butter cups and peanut butter chips, if desired. Totally optional but totally recommended!

If you don't want to enjoy this mousse right away, it is also very good when chilled. It keeps well the fridge for several days.

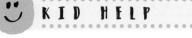 **KID HELP**

- Show your child how the coconut cream separates from the coconut water in the can.
- Let your child mix the coconut cream with the peanut butter, add maple syrup, and adjust sweetness to their liking.
- Let them add the peanut butter cups and chips to their serving.

ALMOND BUTTER MOUSSE

This fluffy deliciousness is the perfect treat for after dinner or a mid-afternoon snack. A serving of almond butter contains a generous amount of magnesium, making this heart-healthy snack a total win!

Serves 2 to 4

1 (15-ounce) can organic full-fat coconut milk, refrigerated for 24 hours

1/2 cup almond butter

3 tablespoons maple syrup

1/4 cup almond milk

Scoop out coconut cream from the can and discard water, or save for later to use in smoothies. Place in a chilled bowl and whip the cream using a hand mixer.

In a small saucepan on medium heat, add almond butter, syrup, and milk; stir to combine and heat until warmed through. Remove from heat and pour into a separate bowl. Fold in coconut whip until well-combined. Place in the refrigerator and let firm up at least 1 hour before serving.

KID HELP

- Show your child how the coconut cream separates from the water in the can when it solidifies in the fridge.
- Let them help you fold together the almond butter and coconut cream.
- When ready to serve, let them top with some extra coconut whip, fresh berries, or a dark chocolate drizzle.

WALNUT PUDDING

This pudding is not only a creamy dream, it's loaded with omega-3 which makes this the ultimate brain food. When eating this power food, you're fueling yourself and your family with antioxidants and so many other vitamins and minerals our bodies crave. Whoever said eating healthy was boring clearly hasn't met the walnut.

Serves 2

4 pitted Medjool dates

1 cup coconut milk

1 cup walnuts, plus extra

1 tablespoon maple syrup, or more to taste

Shredded coconut, cacao nibs, melted dark chocolate, if desired

Place the dates, milk, walnuts, and syrup into a blender or food processor and blend until smooth and creamy.

Pour into a Mason jar or bowl and place in the refrigerator for 10 minutes to set. The colder it gets the thicker it becomes. To make more of the pudding simply double this recipe. Top with coconut, cacao nibs, walnut pieces, or a drizzle of dark chocolate.

 **KID HELP**

- Have your child place everything in the blender then let them hit the on button. Make sure the lid is on securely.
- Let them top the pudding with desired toppings.

SODA-LESS FLOATS

A healthy twist on a classic fave, this float is a creamy refreshment that gives you just the right amount of fizz paired with the perfect amount of better-for-you ingredients.

Serves 2

2 large ripe bananas, frozen

1/4 cup coconut milk

2 tablespoons maple syrup

1 1/2 tablespoons cocoa powder or cacao powder

1 teaspoon peppermint extract

1/3 cup almond milk

Coconut Whipped Cream (page 196), optional

Fresh cherries, optional

Dairy-free chocolate chips, or dark chocolate drizzle, optional

If your bananas aren't already frozen, cut into coins and place bananas in a ziplock bag or glass bowl and put in the freezer for at least 2 hours. Typically I like leaving them there overnight.

Once the bananas are frozen, place them into a food processor or high-powered blender and blend until creamy, scraping down sides of bowl or blender as needed. Add the coconut milk and syrup and give it a good blitz or pulse.

Halfway fill 2 (8-ounce) cups with the banana soft serve.

Blend the cocoa powder, peppermint extract, and almond milk in the remaining banana mixture until thick, creamy, and frothy. Pour mixture over the banana soft serve in the serving cups. It will have the consistency of a soda float that's slightly melted.

Top with Coconut Whipped Cream, fresh cherries, and chocolate chips, if desired. Serve immediately.

 **KID HELP**

- Let your child help you make the banana ice cream by putting the ingredients into the food processor or blender.
- Assemble the floats together. Stick some straws in your floats when they're done and top with desired toppings!

THE MOST DELICIOUS VEGAN CHOCOLATE CHIP COOKIES

Nix the eggs and butter for healthier, better ingredients, and indulge in the chewiest, softest vegan chocolate chip cookies ever!

Makes 2 dozen cookies

1/2 cup coconut oil, melted, at room temperature

1 cup brown sugar or coconut sugar

1/4 cup unsweetened almond milk

2 teaspoons vanilla extract

2 cups whole-wheat pastry flour

1 teaspoon baking soda

1 teaspoon baking powder

1/2 to 1 teaspoon Himalayan pink rock salt

1 cup dairy-free chocolate chips

1/2 cup walnut pieces, optional

Preheat oven to 350 degrees. Line a large baking sheet with parchment paper.

In a large mixing bowl, cream together the oil and sugar. Add the milk and vanilla; mix until creamy.

In a separate bowl, sift together the flour, baking soda, baking powder, and salt. Mix dry ingredients into wet ingredients until well-combined. Fold in chocolate chips and walnuts, if using.

Roll tablespoon-size portions of the dough into balls. Place on baking sheet and gently flatten with the palm of your hand or the back of a spatula. Bake for 8–10 minutes. Mine are perfect at 8 minutes, but ovens vary. Remove from baking sheet and let cool on a wire rack.

Serve immediately or keep stored in an airtight container for up to 1 week.

KID HELP

- Have your kids taste test the dough—it's safe do with this recipe.
- Have your kids help you through the whole process by adding the ingredients to the bowl and then mixing them up.
- Give the kids some dough and have them form their own cookie dough balls to place on the baking sheet.

ICEBOX CAKE

This dream-come-true dessert is layered with vegan graham crackers, softened by chocolate pudding filling, and topped with fresh Coconut Whipped Cream (page 196), making this layered cake impressively amazing without ever having to turn on the oven.

Serves 9

2 1/2 cups almond milk, divided

3 tablespoons cornstarch

1/4 cup cocoa powder or cacao powder

1/4 cup maple or brown rice syrup

Pinch of salt

1 teaspoon vanilla extract

1/2 cup dairy-free chocolate chips

27 to 30 squares vegan graham crackers (4 graham cracker sheets per layer)

Coconut Whipped Cream (page 196), optional

Healthy Chocolate Sauce (page 198), optional

In a small bowl, whisk together 1/2 cup milk and cornstarch. Set aside 5 minutes.

In a medium saucepan over medium heat, add the remaining milk, cocoa powder, syrup, and salt. Whisk to combine. When the mixture is hot, add the cornstarch slurry and bring to a boil; stirring frequently. Reduce to a simmer until pudding starts to thicken. Remove from heat, add vanilla and chocolate chips. Stir until chocolate has melted and pudding is creamy. Let cool for 10 minutes before assembling the cake.

In an 8 x 8-inch baking dish, place 8 to 10 graham cracker squares in the bottom. Pour 1 cup of pudding over the crackers. Add another layer of crackers and the remaining pudding. Add a final layer of crackers.

Chill, covered, in refrigerator for at least 2 hours or overnight. Top with whipped cream and chocolate sauce.

Note: To double this recipe, use a 9 x 13-inch baking dish and double the ingredients for the pudding and graham crackers.

 **KID HELP**

- Let your kids help you prep with the pudding.
- Have them help layer the graham crackers and pudding.
- For the best part, let your child lick the pudding bowl.

BANANA-WALNUT BREAD WITH MAPLE-PECAN FROSTING

I pimped out my favorite banana bread by adding walnuts (brain food) and a to-die-for maple-pecan frosting. Made in 30 minutes, devoured in seconds.

Serves 8 to 10

Bread

1³/₄ cups whole-wheat pastry flour

1¹/₂ teaspoons baking powder

1 teaspoon baking soda

4 medium ripe bananas, mashed

²/₃ cup maple syrup

¹/₃ cup coconut oil, melted

¹/₃ cup unsweetened almond milk

1¹/₂ teaspoons vanilla extract

²/₃ cup walnut pieces

Maple-Pecan Frosting

1 cup chopped pecans, plus extra

¹/₃ cup maple syrup

2 tablespoons coconut oil, melted

1 teaspoon vanilla extract

¹/₃ cup water

Bread

Preheat oven to 350 degrees. Spray a standard loaf pan with nonstick cooking spray.

In a large bowl, whisk together the flour, baking powder, and baking soda. In a separate bowl, whisk together the bananas, syrup, oil, milk, and vanilla. Mix wet ingredients into dry ingredients until well-combined. Fold in walnuts.

Pour batter into loaf pan and bake for 30–35 minutes, or until a toothpick inserted into the center comes out clean. Remove from oven and cool in pan for 10 minutes. Transfer to a wire rack and cool completely before frosting.

Maple-Pecan Frosting

Add 1 cup pecans, syrup, oil, vanilla, and water to a blender or processor and run until smooth and creamy. Place in the refrigerator for 20 minutes to chill and firm up. Spread over banana bread and top with extra pecan pieces.

KID HELP

- Have your child help mix the ingredients.
- Let your child pour the batter into loaf pan.
- Let the kids frost the bread.

SUPER FUDGY BROWNIES

These flourless brownies are decadently fudgy with every bite! This is a classic, staple dessert that will satisfy that chocoholic craving, but on a healthier note.

Serves 9

3 flax eggs (page 23)

4 ounces dark chocolate or dairy-free chocolate chips

$1/2$ cup coconut oil

$1/4$ cup cocoa or cacao powder

$3/4$ cup maple syrup, brown rice syrup, or agave nectar

$1/3$ cup chopped walnuts, optional

Dairy-free chocolate chips, optional

Preheat oven to 350 degrees. Line an 8 x 8-inch baking dish with parchment paper or spray with nonstick cooking spray.

Prepare the flax eggs and pop them in the refrigerator while you melt the chocolate and coconut oil in a small saucepan over low heat. Once melted, pour into a bowl with the flax eggs, cocoa powder, syrup, and walnuts, if using, and mix until well-combined.

Pour batter into baking dish, and bake for 25–30 minutes. Remove from oven and immediately top with chocolate chips, if desired. Let cool in pan for 10 minutes. Once cooled, cut into 9 squares and enjoy with some almond milk!

KID HELP

- Have your child prepare the flax eggs. Teach them what it is and how it works just like eggs would in a recipe.
- Let your child help you mix up all the ingredients. Again, licking bowls and spoons are required.
- Let your child top with chocolate chips before popping into the oven.

CLASSIC CHOCOLATE CAKE WITH CHOCOLATE BUTTERCREAM

This is my go-to chocolate cake because I am indeed a gal who is about all things chocolate. This has alternating layers of super moist chocolate cake filled and frosted with the creamiest chocolate buttercream ever . . . and it's all VEGAN!

Serves 6

2 cups all-purpose flour

$1/2$ cup plus 1 tablespoon cocoa powder

2 teaspoons baking powder

$1^1/2$ teaspoons baking soda

3 tablespoons cornstarch

Pinch of salt

$1/2$ cup melted coconut oil

$1/2$ cup applesauce

1 tablespoon vanilla extract

$1/2$ cup maple syrup

$1^1/2$ cups almond milk

$1/2$ cup water

1 recipe Classic Vegan Chocolate Buttercream (page 200)

Preheat oven to 350 degrees. Prepare 2 (8-inch) round baking pans or springform pans with nonstick cooking spray.

In a large bowl, whisk together the flour, cocoa powder, baking powder, baking soda, cornstarch, and salt. In a medium bowl whisk together the oil, applesauce, vanilla, syrup, milk, and water.

Pour wet ingredients into the dry ingredients and mix until combined. Divide batter between pans and bake for 40 minutes, or until a toothpick inserted in the center comes out clean. Remove from oven and cool completely before frosting.

Place 1 cake on a cake plate and spread buttercream to the edge. Top with second cake and remaining buttercream.

Note: Pop cooled cakes into the freezer for 10 minutes to reduce crumbs when you frost them. You can substitute $1/2$ cup coffee for the $1/2$ cup water. Alternatively, you can use my Classic Vegan Vanilla Buttercream (page 199), or Coconut Whipped Cream (page 196) for frosting as well.

KID HELP

- Let your child help you mix the cake.
- Let your child help pour the batter into the pans.
- Lick all bowls and spoons as desired.

SPLURGE ALERT

CHOCOLATE PEANUT BUTTER PARFAIT

Chocolate and peanut butter are a match made in heaven if you ask me. Pairing these two up and layering them between graham crackers is just genius! It's super easy to put together, so you can have this ready in just minutes!

Serves 4

Graham Cracker Crumble

20 vegan graham cracker sheets (about 2 cups if you use ready-made crumbs)

4 tablespoons cacao powder

$1/2$ cup melted vegan butter

Peanut Butter Mousse

2 (15-ounce) cans full fat coconut milk, refrigerated for 24 hours

5 tablespoons maple syrup

$1/2$ cup unsalted creamy peanut butter

1 teaspoon Himalayan pink rock salt

Peanuts, optional

Preheat oven to 350 degrees. Lightly spray a baking sheet with nonstick cooking spray.

Graham Cracker Crumble

In a food processor, pulse crackers until they become crumbs, about 1 minute. Place crumbs, cacao powder, and butter into a bowl and mix until moist and crumbly.

Spread evenly across baking sheet. Bake for 15 minutes, or longer for extra crunch.

Peanut Butter Mousse

Scoop coconut cream from cans and discard water, or save for later use. Place in a large bowl and beat on medium speed until smooth with a whipped consistency. Add the syrup and peanut butter. Mix on high speed until well-combined.

In 4 (8- to 16-ounce) glasses, add a layer of crumble and then a layer of mousse. Repeat layers until glasses are filled. Top with peanuts, if desired.

Note: Substitute any nut butter for the peanut butter. Use the mousse right away or store in the refrigerator for up to 4 days. For a desired mousse consistency, whip it back up with a hand mixer or spoon. This mousse recipe is also ideal for frosting cakes or cupcakes.

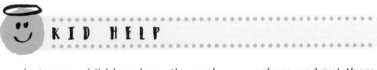

KID HELP

- Let your child break up the graham crackers and put them in the processor.
- Have them help you whip together the peanut butter mousse.
- Have them assemble their own parfait.

SPLURGE ALERT

OATMEAL CREAM PIES

This is hands down my favorite dessert. Soft oatmeal cookies sandwiched together with a sweet vegan buttercream makes these simply sensational.

Makes 24 cream pies

1 1/2 cups all-purpose flour

1 teaspoon baking soda

1/2 teaspoon baking powder

1 teaspoon cinnamon

1 cup rolled oats

Pinch of salt

2 flax eggs (page 23)

1/2 cup vegan butter, melted

1/2 cup cane sugar

1/2 cup brown or coconut sugar

1/2 cup applesauce

1 tablespoon maple syrup

1 teaspoon vanilla extract

1 cup raisins, optional

Cream Filling

1/2 cup vegan butter, softened

1/2 cup vegan shortening

3 cups powdered sugar

1 teaspoon vanilla extract

1/4 cup almond milk

Preheat oven to 350 degrees. Line a baking sheet with parchment paper and spray with nonstick cooking spray.

In a small bowl, whisk together the flour, baking soda, baking powder, cinnamon, oats, and salt. In a large bowl, beat the flax eggs, butter, and sugars until fluffy. Add the applesauce, syrup, and vanilla and mix until combined. Add wet ingredients to dry ingredients and mix until just combined. Fold in raisins, if using.

Drop dough by rounded tablespoons, 2 inches apart, on baking sheet. Bake for 10 minutes. Remove from oven and cool before transferring to a wire rack. Cool completely before filling.

Cream Filling

Place butter and shortening in a large bowl and cream together until fluffy. Add sugar, 1 cup at a time, and then mix on high speed for 3 minutes. Add the vanilla and milk and mix on high for 5 minutes, or until sugar has dissolved. Scrape down sides of bowl if needed.

Spread filling on the bottom of 1 cookie and top with another cookie. Repeat with remaining cookies.

KID HELP

- Have your child help mix dough and place on baking sheet.
- Let them help make the filling, and sandwich their own cookies together.

CHOCOLATE AND PEANUT BUTTER OATMEAL BARS

These perfectly proportioned thick, creamy, soft, and chewy bars are truly magical. Topped with melted dairy-free chocolate, this is a trio you need not go without. Perfect for breakfast, a snack, or an after dinner treat.

Makes 12 to 16 bars

1/2 cup vegan butter

1 flax egg (page 23)

1/2 cup unsweetened shredded coconut

1/3 cup brown sugar or coconut sugar

1 teaspoon vanilla extract

1 teaspoon baking soda

1/3 cup peanut butter, plus extra

1 cup whole-wheat flour

1 cup rolled oats

1/2 cup vegan butter

1/2 cup dairy-free chocolate chips

Preheat oven to 350 degrees. Line a standard baking sheet with parchment paper and spray with nonstick cooking spray.

In a large bowl add the butter, flax egg, coconut, sugar, vanilla, baking soda, and peanut butter. Mix well. (If your peanut butter is not as runny as you'd like, warm it up in a saucepan with some coconut oil.) Fold in flour and oats; mix to combine.

Spread evenly over baking sheet and bake for 15–20 minutes. Remove from oven and immediately sprinkle chocolate chips over the top. The heat will melt them down nicely. You can leave them as is, or using an offset spatula, smooth out the chocolate.

Place in the freezer for 10 minutes to set the chocolate. Remove and top with extra chocolate chips and a drizzle of peanut butter, if desired. Cut into bars. Store on the counter or in the fridge in an airtight container for up to 4 days.

KID HELP

- Let your child help measure out the ingredients.
- Give the batter a good mix then let them help you spread it across the baking sheet.
- Let the kids sprinkle the chocolate chips on top and watch them melt.

STRAWBERRY CHEESECAKE

I seriously have never loved cheesecake more until now. It's like awesome went into a bowl, baked for a bit, and came out even more awesome! That's how amazing this is.

Serves 6 to 8

Crust

10 vegan graham cracker sheets

2 tablespoons coconut sugar

2 tablespoons coconut butter, melted

4 teaspoons water

Filling

1 1/2 cups almond meal or flour

1/4 cup agave nectar

1 teaspoon vanilla extract

1 teaspoon almond extract

1 tablespoon lemon juice

4 tablespoons coconut butter, melted

1/2 cup water

Topping

1 cup fresh strawberries, hulled and sliced

1/2 cup strawberry jam

Sliced almonds

Preheat oven to 350 degrees. Spray a 9-inch round baking pan or springform pan with coconut oil spray.

Crust

Place crackers in a food processor and pulse until crumbly. Add the sugar, butter, and water, and pulse until well-combined. Press crumbs evenly into the bottom and halfway up the sides of pan. Make for 10 minutes. Remove and cool.

Filling

In a clean food processor or blender, add all the filling ingredients. Blend until smooth and creamy. Pour filling over crust and bake for 20 minutes. Remove and let cool on rack for 20 minutes.

Topping

Arrange strawberries over cheesecake, covering the top completely. Heat the jam and pour over the strawberries. Sprinkle almonds over top. Chill for 1 hour before serving.

KID HELP

- Let your child help make the crust and press into the pan.
- Let them hull the strawberries. You can use a straw to hull the strawberries by placing the straw at the bottom and gently pushing through, aiming for the green stem or leaves at the top. The stem will pop out with one push.

ALMOND BUTTER-CHOCOLATE PUDDING PIE

This pie will have everyone coming back for seconds, even thirds! The decadently creamy ultra-thick almond butter and chocolate pudding center over the chocolatey cookie crust is a 5-star winner!

Serves 6

25 to 28 Oreo cookies

5 to 6 tablespoons vegan butter, melted

$1/2$ cup full-fat coconut cream

1 cup dairy-free chocolate chips

1 teaspoon vanilla extract

1 tablespoon cornstarch

Pinch of salt

$1/2$ cup creamy almond butter

$1/2$ cup vegan butter, melted

8 ounces vegan cream cheese

1 cup powdered sugar

1 recipe Coconut Whipped Cream (page 196)

Drizzle of dark chocolate

Toasted coconut shreds, optional

Sliced almonds, optional

Preheat oven to 350 degrees. Lightly spray a 9- or 10-inch pie pan with nonstick cooking spray.

Place the whole cookies and butter into a food processor and pulse until cookies are reduced to fine crumbs. Transfer to pie pan, pressing evenly on the bottom and up the sides a bit. Bake for 10 minutes and cool completely before adding the filling.

In a saucepan over medium heat, bring the coconut cream to a boil. Remove from heat and pour over chocolate chips; add vanilla, cornstarch, and salt and stir until chocolate is melted and smooth. Pour over cookie crust refrigerate for 30 minutes to set.

In a medium bowl, whip together the almond butter, butter, cream cheese, and sugar. Pour mixture over the chocolate filling. Top with whipped cream, chocolate drizzle, coconut, and almonds, if desired. Refrigerate to set for at least 2 hours or overnight.

Note: Use a ready-made vegan pie crust in place of the cookie crust; prebake according to package direction.

KID HELP

- Have your child help press crust into pie pan.
- Have them help make the fillings and pour each layer.

NO-BAKE OREO COOKIE CHEESECAKES

The cookie-to-cheesecake ratio is so on-point in this recipe that with every bite comes a flavor explosion of Oreo cheesecake deliciousness. It will easily impress, and leave people wondering how is this really vegan!

Serves 12

Crust

10 Oreo cookies

1 tablespoon vegan butter, melted

Crust

Place the whole cookies in a food processor or blender and pulse until reduced to fine crumbs. Add the butter and mix well to combine.

Prepare a 12-cup muffin pan by cutting strips of parchment paper and pressing them into the bottom and up the sides of each muffin cup, leaving a tab on each side. This will make it easy to pull out the cheesecakes when set.

Press about 2 tablespoons of crumb mixture into each muffin cup, making sure the strips of paper are set in place. Place the pan in refrigerator to chill.

Filling

1 1/2 cups cashews, soaked for 2–4 hours

1/2 cup coconut cream

1/3 cup coconut oil

1/3 cup rice malt syrup

1 teaspoon vanilla extract

Juice from 1/2 lemon

Pinch of Himalayan pink rock salt

1 recipe Coconut Whipped Cream (page 196)

8 Oreo cookies, crushed, plus extra

Filling

Add filling ingredients, except cookies, into a blender or processor and run until smooth and creamy. Pour filling into a bowl and fold in crushed cookies. Fill muffin cups evenly with filling and place in the freezer to set for at least 4 hours.

Remove from freezer and let thaw for 5 minutes before lifting out of pan. To serve, top with Coconut Whipped Cream and extra cookie pieces, if desired. Stores well in the refrigerator for up to 4 days.

KID HELP

- Have your child get all the ingredients ready with you.
- Let the kids press crust into muffin cups.
- Have them place filling ingredients in the blender.

DIPS, SAUCES, AND STAPLES

"SOMETHING TO FALL BACK ON"

These are my go-to dips, sauces, and staples like sour cream and cheeses. I make them weekly with my family as they are easy to store and can play many roles in different recipes, giving us variety. Each recipe is versatile and will keep you from wondering what you should make for dinner on a busy night. And desserts, we can't forget about desserts! With these recipes on hand, you'll always have a nutritious something to fall back on.

VEGAN SOUR CREAM

This vegan sour cream is velvety smooth and delightfully rich and tasty. Try this on any Mexican dish, salads, or on sandwiches in place of mayo. It is a nice vegan twist on traditional sour cream.

Makes 2 cups

1 (14-ounce) package organic firm silken tofu

Juice of 1 lemon (about 3 tablespoons)

2 tablespoons extra virgin olive oil

1 tablespoon water

1 teaspoon apple cider vinegar

1 teaspoon yellow or Dijon mustard

1 teaspoon onion powder

1 teaspoon garlic powder

Salt and pepper, to taste

Using your hands, crumble the tofu into a blender. Add the lemon juice, oil, water, vinegar, mustard, onion powder, and garlic powder, and season with salt and pepper. Blend until smooth and creamy, about 2 minutes.

Taste and adjust seasonings to your liking.

Keep stored in a glass jar with an airtight lid for up to 7 days in the fridge.

Note: After blending, you can fold in 1 tablespoon of chopped fresh dill, rosemary, chives, and/or green onion.

 KID HELP

- Once you drain the tofu, let your child crumble it up with their hands and place in the blender.
- Let them help you add all other ingredients then hit the on button to get the creamy vegan sour cream party started.

SUPER EASY TZATZIKI SAUCE

This version of the Greek classic is healthy, vegan, and gluten free. It's an ample dip best served with an endless amount of veggies, pita bread, or crackers.

Makes 2½ cups

1 cup raw cashews, soaked for 2–4 hours or flash soaked (see note)

4 tablespoons lemon juice

2 tablespoons tahini

2 cloves garlic

2 tablespoons hemp seeds

Salt and pepper, to taste

7 tablespoons water (give or take)

1 cucumber, diced

1 tablespoon fresh or dried dill

1 tablespoon dried parsley

½ tablespoon fresh or dried mint, optional

Drain and rinse the cashews.

In a food processor or blender, add cashews, lemon juice, tahini, garlic, hemp seeds, and water; season with salt and pepper. Run until smooth and creamy, scraping down the sides with a rubber spatula as necessary.

Transfer to a large mixing bowl. Add the cucumber, dill, parsley, mint, and season with more salt and pepper. Mix well. Taste and adjust seasonings as desired.

Serve with salads, falafel, or simply as a dipping sauce for veggies. Enjoy!

Keeps well in an airtight container in the fridge for up to 5 days.

Note: If you don't want to wait hours for the cashews to soak, you can flash soak them! Boil enough water to cover the cashews, remove from heat, add the cashews, and let sit in the hot water for 15–30 minutes.

 KID HELP

- Let your child add all ingredients into the processor or blender and run until smooth.
- When you're scraping down the sides, let your child do the tasting to see if any adjustments are needed.

CASHEW RICOTTA CHEESE

Cashews are a great source of magnesium and zinc; minerals that are uber important for our muscles and bones. The cashews make this cheese not only wonderfully tasty but nutritionally dense. Great on pastas, pizza, or as a dip. Double, triple win!

Makes 2 to 3 cups

2 cups raw cashews, soaked for 2–4 hours or flash soaked (see note)

1 cup water

Juice of 1 lemon (about 3 tablespoons)

2 cloves garlic

4 tablespoons nutritional yeast

1 tablespoon onion powder

Sea salt, to taste

Drain and rinse the cashews.

Place all the ingredients in a high-speed blender; blend until just smooth but slightly crumbly. You want it to have the same texture as ricotta cheese.

Serve over pasta, on pizza, or as a dip for veggies and chips.

Store in the fridge in a tightly sealed glass jar for up to 2 weeks. Be sure to put a date on it.

Note: If you don't want to wait hours for the cashews to soak, you can flash soak them! Boil enough water to cover the cashews, remove from heat, add the cashews, and let sit in the hot water for 15–30 minutes.

 **K I D   H E L P**

- Let your kids drain and rinse the cashews.
- Have them place the ingredients in a high-speed blender and run it until smooth and creamy.
- Have them taste and approve by dipping in fresh broccoli florets, celery, or carrot sticks.

DELICIOUSLY EASY VEGAN PARMESAN CHEESE

You'll want to go ahead and make this in huge batches at a time because you'll put it on just about everything. The ingredients are simple, and it will make anything savory taste even better.

Makes 2 cups

1 cup raw cashews

¼ cup nutritional yeast

2 tablespoons hemp seeds

2 tablespoons sesame seeds

1 heaping tablespoon garlic powder

Salt and pepper, to taste

Add all the ingredients to a food processor; run until crumbly. Adjust seasonings to your liking if needed.

Store in the fridge in a glass jar with lid for up to 1 month. Be sure to put a date on it.

Note: Almonds or any other nut you fancy can be subbed for cashews.

 **KID HELP**

- Let your child help measure out the ingredients then place in food processor and run until crumbly.
- Let them taste and adjust seasonings to their liking.

VEGAN PESTO

Kale was crowned king of all greens, and in this recipe it definitely holds up to its prestigious title. This super green is packed with vitamin B and C, which promotes iron absorption. I love using this pesto on sandwiches and in pastas.

Makes 1 ½ cups

⅓ cup chopped fresh basil leaves

¼ cup pine nuts, almonds, or walnuts

1 to 2 cloves garlic

1 cup chopped kale

¼ cup extra virgin olive oil

Salt and pepper, to taste

Place all ingredients into a food processor or blender; pulse until combined. Serve over pasta or spread it on sandwiches.

KID HELP

- Have your child help measure out all ingredients and add to the processor or blender and pulse until combined.
- Have them do a taste test to see if the seasoning is just right.

THE BEST VEGAN CHEESE WIZ

Don't let the awesome cheese-like consistency fool you, this good-for-you cheese wiz is high in beta-carotene and Vitamin C. You can feel good about getting your healthy snacking on with this by pouring it over your favorite meals, dipping in your fave veggies, or, to get even more creative, turning it into a warming soup!

Makes 2 to 3 cups

4 cups halved red potatoes

$1^1/2$ cups large-dice carrots

$^1/2$ cup water

$^1/3$ cup extra virgin olive oil

$^1/2$ cup nutritional yeast

1 tablespoon lemon juice

1 tablespoon onion powder

1 tablespoon garlic powder

1 tablespoon dried parsley

Salt and pepper, to taste

Steam or boil the potatoes and carrots until tender.

Place all ingredients into a high-speed blender and run until smooth and creamy. Scrape down the sides with a rubber spatula if necessary.

Taste and adjust seasoning to your liking.

Pour over pasta, fries, vegetables, or eat it straight up because it's that good.

Store in an airtight container in the fridge for up to 5 days. When it cools, it will firm up. Reheat for a few minutes to get it back to being smooth and creamy.

 KID HELP

- Let your child help you prep the carrots and potatoes.
- Once all the ingredients are ready, let them help add to the blender.
- Show them the consistency and let them taste the savory deliciousness.

VEGAN ALFREDO SAUCE

Be ready to eat this by the spoonful because the taste is beyond yum-tastic. Made with almond milk and some seasonings and spices, this will rev up any meal whether it's pasta or poured over roasted broccoli or cauliflower.

Makes 2½ cups

- 2½ cups unsweetened almond milk
- 2½ tablespoons brown rice flour
- 1½ tablespoons nutritional yeast
- 1½ teaspoons Bragg Liquid Aminos or low-sodium soy sauce
- 1 tablespoon garlic powder
- 1 tablespoon onion powder
- 2 tablespoons vegan butter
- 1 teaspoon yellow mustard
- 1 teaspoon Himalayan pink salt

In a medium saucepan over medium-low heat, whisk all the ingredients together for 5 minutes.

Reduce heat to a simmer and stir frequently for 8–10 minutes until it starts to thicken. Once thick, remove from heat.

Serve over your favorite pasta and add any vegetable of choice, like broccoli or peas!

KID HELP

- Let your child stand with you as you add in the ingredients to the saucepan. Show them how it starts to thicken and becomes extra creamy in consistency.
- Let them taste it by pouring it over their fave pasta dish or having them dip their fave veggies in it.

MY GO-TO CARAMEL SAUCE

Made with only five ingredients, this sauce will add sweet flavor to any snack, dessert, or dish your heart desires. It's thick, creamy, sweet, and just the right amount of salty.

Makes 1½ cups

1 (14-ounce) can full-fat coconut milk

½ cup coconut sugar

1 tablespoon coconut oil, melted

Pinch of Himalayan pink salt

1 teaspoon vanilla extract

In a medium saucepan over medium heat, combine the coconut milk and sugar. Whisk together until well-incorporated, and bring to a boil, stirring frequently.

Once mixture comes to a boil, reduce heat to low and boil slowly for about an hour. Using a rubber spatula, keep stirring so the bottom doesn't burn. Scrape down the sides as needed. The caramel will reduce and start to thicken.

Remove from heat and whisk in the oil, salt, and vanilla.

Let cool to room temperature, stirring occasionally. The caramel will continue to thicken as it cools.

Once cooled, transfer to a glass jar with a lid, date it, and store it in the fridge. Lasts for up to 2 weeks.

Put it on anything!

KID HELP

- Let your child help you whisk this sauce into thickness.
- Have your child date the jar you are using to keep track of when it was made.

COCONUT WHIPPED CREAM

This is a heart–healthy, delectable whipped cream you can use on desserts or serve up with fresh fruit. It's a staple in vegan, dairy-free living and will make its way into many sweet treats.

Makes 1 cup

- 1 (14-ounce) can full-fat coconut milk, refrigerated for 24 hours
- 3 tablespoons maple syrup
- 1 teaspoon vanilla extract

The coconut milk needs to be refrigerated before use in order to whip properly. When refrigerated, it solidifies and the cream separates from the water. Scoop out the cream for whipping, and save the water for later use in smoothies.

Chill a mixing bowl and beaters in the freezer for 10 minutes prior to whipping.

Place cream in chilled bowl and beat with a mixer until smooth and creamy. Add in the syrup and vanilla and mix well. Taste and adjust sweetness as desired.

Note: For a sweeter cream, you can add $1/2$ cup organic powdered sugar.

To make more, simply double or triple the recipe!

KID HELP

- Show your child how the water and cream separate from each other when left in the fridge overnight.
- Scoop out the cream and let your child add in the other ingredients.
- Have them mix it up and dip in their fave fruit for a taste test.

HEALTHY CHOCOLATE SAUCE

Honestly, who doesn't love a little dark chocolate drizzle on basically anything dessert related? But this isn't your average dark chocolate. Cacao is a high source of plant-based iron and has forty times the antioxidants of blueberries.

Makes about ⅓ cup

- 2 tablespoons cacao or cocoa powder
- 2 tablespoons coconut oil, melted
- 2 tablespoons maple syrup

Place all ingredients in a bowl and mix well. To make more chocolate, simply double or triple this recipe as needed.

 **KID HELP**

- Give your child a bowl and the ingredients and let them have at it.
- Licking utensils required.

CLASSIC VEGAN VANILLA BUTTERCREAM

This vegan buttercream is fluffy, smooth, and easy to make. It will take your desserts and snacks to the next level of goodness.

Makes 1¾ cups

- ½ cup vegan butter, room temperature
- ½ cup vegan shortening, room temperature
- 4 cups powdered sugar
- 1 teaspoon vanilla extract
- ¼ cup almond milk

Place butter and shortening in the bowl of a stand mixer; cream together until nice and fluffy.

Add sugar, 1 cup at a time. Once all the sugar has been added, turn on high speed for 3 minutes.

Add the vanilla and milk, continuing to mix on high for 5 minutes until all the sugar has dissolved. Use a rubber spatula to scrape down the sides of the bowl as needed.

If using on cupcakes, cakes, or cookies, store according to dessert. If storing buttercream alone, it will keep up to 5 days in the fridge in an air-tight container. It will also firm up a bit in the fridge, so let come to room temperature and give it a stir before using.

KID HELP

- Let your child help you add the ingredients to the stand mixer.
- If you need a taste tester, no one is better than your kids. If it needs to be sweetened a little more they will tell you.
- Have your kids help frost the dessert you are making.

CLASSIC VEGAN CHOCOLATE BUTTERCREAM

This vegan chocolate buttercream is extra crazy, but so am I! You'd be doing your baked goods a disservice if you didn't add this to it. Fluffy, thick, rich, and creamy, it is a must make for all my chocolate lovers.

Makes 1¾ cups

- ½ cup vegan butter, room temperature
- ½ cup vegan shortening, room temperature
- 4 cups powdered sugar
- ½ cup cacao or cocoa powder
- 1 teaspoon vanilla extract
- ¼ cup almond milk

Place butter and shortening in the bowl of a stand mixer; cream together until nice and fluffy.

Add sugar 1 cup at a time. Add cacao powder. Once the cacao powder has been added, turn on high speed for 3 minutes.

Add the vanilla and milk, continuing to mix on high for 5 minutes until all the sugar has dissolved. Use a rubber spatula to scrape down the sides of the bowl as needed.

If using on cupcakes, cakes, or cookies, store according to dessert. If storing buttercream alone, it will keep up to 5 days in the fridge. You can make this the day before you frost a cake or cupcakes, or you can frost cupcakes the night before serving, just make sure to keep the dessert in the fridge covered with an air-tight lid so it doesn't dry out.

KID HELP

- Let your child help you add the ingredients to the stand mixer.
- Once finished whipping this up, decorate desired desserts together and have fun!

CASHEW DESSERT CREAM

This is my go-to, all-purpose dessert cream. It is so easy and quick to make, and is perfectly paired with sandwich cookies, puddings, or swirled on top of vegan ice cream and smoothie bowls.

Makes about 3 cups

2 cups raw cashews, soaked 2–4 hours or flash soaked (see note)

2 teaspoons vanilla extract

1/4 cup maple syrup, plus extra as needed

1/4 cup almond milk

Drain and rinse the cashews.

Place all the ingredients in a high-speed blender; blend until smooth and creamy.

You can taste and adjust sweetness to your liking by adding 1 tablespoon of maple syrup at a time.

Store in the fridge in an airtight container or a glass jar with lid. Lasts for up to 2 weeks. Be sure to put a date on it.

Goes well with sweet snacks and desserts like cookies, cupcakes, muffins, or fruit.

Note: If you don't want to wait hours for the cashews to soak, you can flash soak them! Boil enough water to cover the cashews, remove from heat, add the cashews, and let sit in the hot water for 15–30 minutes.

KID HELP

- Let your child throw all ingredients into a blender and run until silky smooth.
- Tasting by the spoonful and licking the bowl is required.

INDEX

ABOUT THE AUTHOR

Jennifer Rose Rossano is an author, recipe developer, lifestyle writer, and the content creator behind NeuroticMommy.com. She is a comically worried wife and mom of two boys, a pink smoothie lover, and a yoga and meditation enthusiast.

Jennifer's mission is to provide answers on how to lead a healthier lifestyle. She gives practical tips on everyday living and nutrition, creates easy-to-make plant-based recipes, and is always on the hunt for eco-friendly, cruelty-free products to share with her readers. Her goal is to make life easier for her audience with her trusted opinion, personal life experiences, and expertise. She aims to inspire and motivate. Jennifer believes that being healthy is not just about the foods we eat, but that we should focus on the mind, body, and spirit as a collective whole. She has a passion for supporting women on their journey toward health and happiness not only for themselves but for their families. As quoted in *Thrive Magazine,* "Being or living healthy isn't a style or trend, it's just life and we all deserve that."

METRIC CONVERSION CHART

Volume Measurements		Weight Measurements		Temperature Conversion	
U.S.	Metric	U.S.	Metric	Fahrenheit	Celsius
1 teaspoon	5 ml	$^1/_2$ ounce	15 g	250	120
1 tablespoon	15 ml	1 ounce	30 g	300	150
$^1/_4$ cup	60 ml	3 ounces	90 g	325	160
$^1/_3$ cup	75 ml	4 ounces	115 g	350	180
$^1/_2$ cup	125 ml	8 ounces	225 g	375	190
$^2/_3$ cup	150 ml	12 ounces	350 g	400	200
$^3/_4$ cup	175 ml	1 pound	450 g	425	220
1 cup	250 ml	$2^1/_4$ pounds	1 kg	450	230